Shopping Cart Pantheism

SHOPPING CART PANTHEISM

Jeanne Randolph

ARP BOOKS • WINNIPEG

Copyright ©2015 Jeanne Randolph

ARP Books (Arbeiter Ring Publishing)
201E-121 Osborne Street
Winnipeg, Manitoba
Canada R3L 1Y4
arpbooks.org

Printed in Canada by Friesens
Design by Mike Carroll
Interior illustrations by Jones Miller

COPYRIGHT NOTICE
This book is fully protected under the copyright laws of Canada and all other countries of the Copyright Union and is subject to royalty. Any properly footnoted quotation of up to five hundred sequential words may be quoted without permission, so long as the total number of words does not exceed two thousand. For longer continuous quotations or for a greater number of words, contact Arbeiter Ring Publishing for permission.

MANITOBA ARTS COUNCIL
CONSEIL DES ARTS DU MANITOBA

Canada Council   Conseil des Arts
for the Arts   du Canada

Canadian   Patrimoine
Heritage   canadien

Manitoba

ARP acknowledges the financial support of our publishing activities by Manitoba Culture, Heritage, and Tourism, and the Government of Canada through the Canada Book Fund.

ARP acknowledges the support of the Province of Manitoba through the Book Publishing Tax Credit and the Book Publisher Marketing Assistance Program.

We acknowledge the support of the Canada Council for our publishing program.

With the generous support of the Manitoba Arts Council.

Printed on paper from 100% recycled post-consumer waste.

LIBRARY AND ARCHIVES CANADA CATALOGUING IN PUBLICATION

Randolph, Jeanne, 1943-, author
    Shopping cart pantheism / Jeanne Randolph ; with
illustrations by Jones Miller.

Includes bibliographical references.
ISBN 978-1-894037-61-7 (pbk.)

    1. Consumption (Economics)--Religious aspects--
Christianity. 2. Advertising--Nevada--Las Vegas--Religious
aspects--Christianity. I. Miller, Jones, 1984-, illustrator II. Title.

BR115.C67R35 2015   241›.68   C2015-901424-7

Contents

9 *Takeoff*

17 Photograph One: *"It's Nice to See You"*

23 Photograph Two: *Travelodge Room 7*

29 Photograph Three: *The Miracle Mile*

35 Photograph Four: *The Eternal City*

45 Photograph Five: *Hells*

51 Photograph Six: *Twentieth Century Rabid Skunk*

55 Photograph Seven: *Dogmatics in Outline*

61 Photograph Eight: *The King*

63 Photograph Nine: *My Hanky*

67 Photograph Ten: *Advertese*

71 Photograph Eleven: *Wee Beasties*

- **77** Photograph Twelve: *Pandemonium*
- **81** Photograph Thirteen: *Dow Jones Concussion*
- **89** Photograph Fourteen: *Being and Thingness*
- **93** Photograph Fifteen: *Under the Monorail*
- **101** Photograph Sixteen: *The Crow and the Fish*
- **109** Photograph Seventeen: *Miss Liberty*
- **115** Photograph Eighteen: *It's All Good*
- **119** Photograph Nineteen: *Second Century CET (Current Era of the Transistor)*
- **127** Photograph Twenty: *The Grim Reaper*
- **131** *Notes*
- **135** *Acknowledgements*

for andrew and jennifer, in gratitude

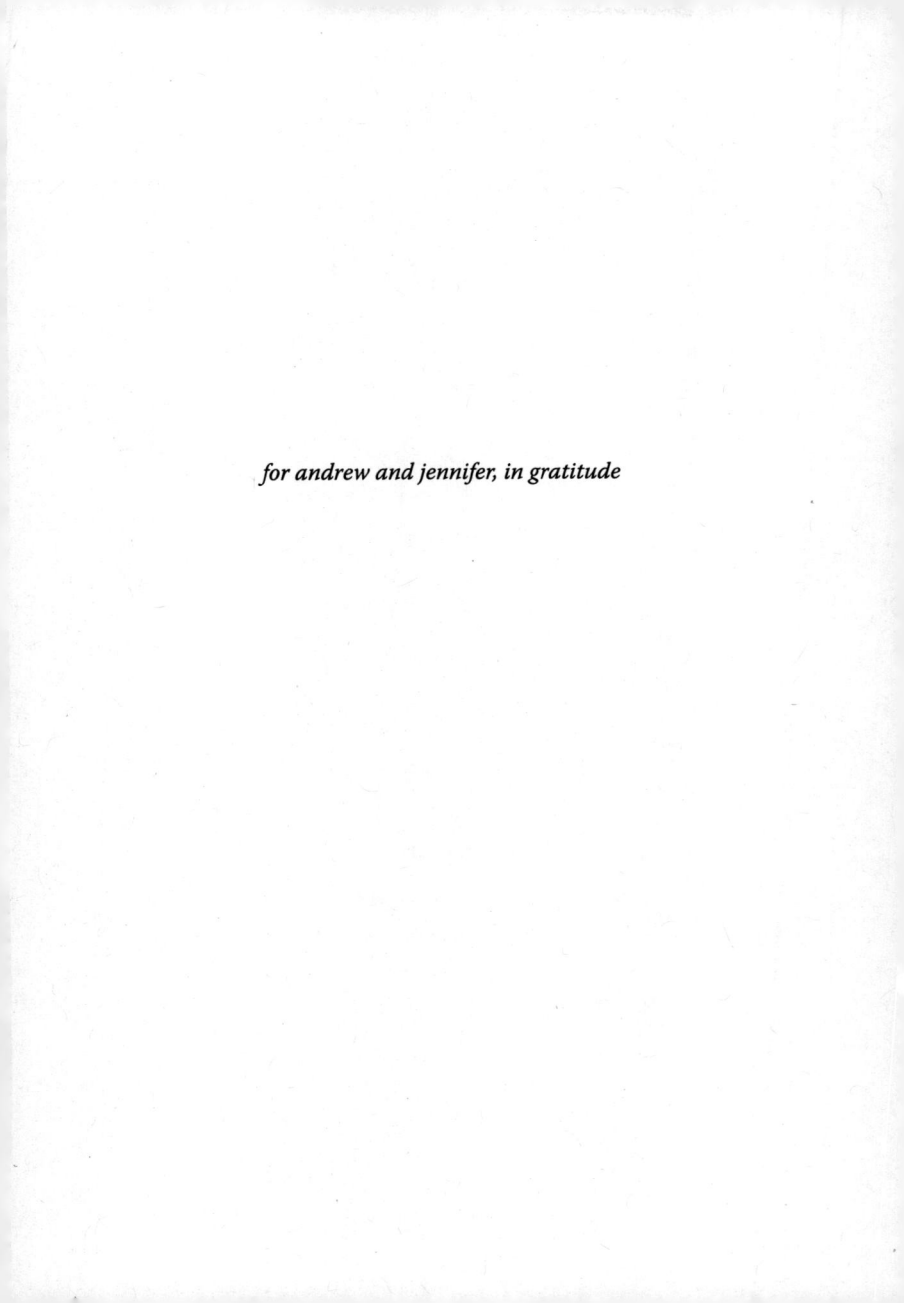

Takeoff

Takeoff and landing are the unhappiest times in an airplane. Takeoff is when I will distract myself with anything in the magazine pouch except the terrifying safety instructions. Years ago flying somewhere, I grabbed a shiny brochure meant to divert me from fear of dying in a fireball. Every page was absolutely stirring. The advertisements in particular were wildly energetic. Every colour was supersaturated: lizard green lipstick, vermillion silk necktie, azure porcelain cat, gold golf ball cufflinks, iridescent purple scarves, even a sterling silver shopping cart brooch. Each product was so vivacious it seemed ready to extrude itself from the page and grab hundred dollar bills right out of my wallet, or to clutch me by my shirt and yank me into its world, a world where objects rule and people succumb.

"Where objects rule and people succumb," I mused. And then I understood. Now is the time to adjust our religious experience to our empty materialism. After one hundred years of mass-produced, mass-mediated overstimulation, the most strenuous ritual our souls can manage is clicking on a shopping cart icon, sometimes pushing an actual shopping cart. We North Americans have inexorably adapted to a glut of merchandise. Advertising is ubiquitous and as normal as toilet paper. I bet every last one of us has been lured into a store and bought stuff. Why not jump right into shopping cart pantheism? There certainly are lots of dandy things to fill a shopping cart. Why don't we commit ourselves to worshipping all of it? Let us welcome all this stuff into a product pantheon. All the things we have, all the things for sale, all the things we could buy. It adds up to divinity on top of divinity. As the philosopher Thales said in the sixth century BCE, "everything is full of gods," which must include shopping carts.

The revelatory airplane ride was six years go. Since then I have studied pantheistic poetry; it is scintillating. I have studied the history of Christianity. It's melodramatic. I studied the work of major theologians 1900 to 1950; it's tedious. It took longer than it should have to recognize that their *apologias* hadn't changed since the fifth century. But these studies had been necessary to write a book, *The Godliness of Goods*. What I am insinuating by the phrase "the godliness of goods" is that our souls are so thin we can't withstand anything transcendent. *The Godliness of Goods* was to have been an analysis of twentieth century culture as it backed away from Christianity and fell into product adoration.

In addition to years of reading, I was betting that self-psychoanalysis would be a promising method to map the route from rote Christianity to commodity pantheism. To write a book on the godliness of goods I had decided I must follow Freud's lead when he wrote *The Interpretation of Dreams*. To gain insight I must sleep. Most dreams are surreal. I convinced myself that the bizarre juxtapositions of objects in a dream would reveal the demonic desires that had enabled consumerism. Just because dreams are nonsense doesn't mean they hold no clues.

Awake and asleep I needed to relive the nightmare of materialism's victory after World War II. As nightmare objects skid and bounce over the dreamscape, would they betray the origins of our lust for overabundance? Advertising may have incubated before World War II, but after the war advertising became a contagion. Consumerism became a compulsion. Was this inevitable? Or does something like mass hysteria explain it? If not hysteria, is there an undiagnosed syndrome? I figured I must unearth the fragments of Christian mythology backed up in the muddiest sediment of my Subconscious. Something had happened to Christianity. It had lost its credibility. After World War II Jesus wasn't Mr. Right anymore, or else our North American psyches had lost the strength to worship anything more edifying than merchandise.

At long last we North Americans are primed to host new deities, especially if the latest deities are *prêt-à-porter*. Commodity pantheism will be a very relaxing form of worship. Consumer goods are everywhere, any and all accessible to be revered 24/7. Product pantheism doesn't require a vision quest, and no baptism, no catechism, no commitment. Product adoration doesn't involve feeling nice toward others; it doesn't even involve the effort of hypocrisy. Shopping cart pantheism is no more communal than applying for a credit card or for bankruptcy. It is no more ritualistic than keying in a PIN. It's as individualistic as ear buds. In other words, no congregation standing up and sitting down simultaneously. No congregation period. We won't be waiting a few hundred years for consumerism to petrify into a religious institution. It isn't going to. And commodity pantheism is perfect for the "God is dead" crowd because consumer items are definitely not alive.

Assuming almost everyone born in North America between 1940 and 1970 is exactly like me, I first pictured consumerism all but annihilating whatever had remained of Christian dogma. My first vision of consumerism resembled a 1950s science fiction movie. Consumerism was enlarging exponentially like molecules from a chunk of fast food. A massive radioactive grease globule would be squishing everything as it rolled over a small mid-Western town. Then, I reconsidered. This scenario was not fully accurate. A revised version was hatched: Christian teachings have not been obliterated by consumerism. It's as if bits of Christianity are being pecked up by the Big Bird of Advertising and processed in his crop. To be less anachronistic, it's as if a ravenous King-Kong-size Woody Woodpecker had emerged from the silver screen and mistaken fragments of the Jesus story for kernels of corn. <u>Christianity has not been destroyed; it has been digested. The crumbs of Christianity have been *metabolized* by consumerism.</u>

"Martin Luther Struck by Lightning"

To intensify an experience of shopping cart pantheism I figured I would visit a city that matched this metabolic metaphor. That is why I decided to spend three days in Las Vegas. Las Vegas would be a major digestive tract to explore. Las Vegas is bloated by object-deities small, medium, and massive. The massive ones are outdoors. Really big, obviously glamorous products would have an astonishing effect on me, and lead me on like a new improved Star of Bethlehem. When I studied the huge outdoor consumer goods their divine attributes would be obvious, and therefore no effort to describe. The most bombastic material gods in Las Vegas would be their sky-high monuments, so I wouldn't have to buy tickets, poker chips, or cocktails to behold them. The conversion experience would be easy. I wouldn't have to stumble around with scabs on my eyes like St. Paul, attend high school in Louisiana like Bobby Jindal, or get struck by lightning like Martin Luther.

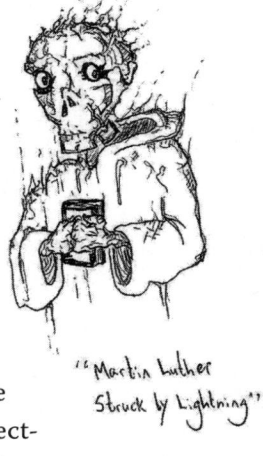

Three days may not seem enough to comprehend the connection between Las Vegas and shopping cart pantheism. It is plenty long enough with an active Subconscious and lots of naptime.

When the plane to Las Vegas was 35,000 feet above sea level I was stricken with self-doubt. Am I the only one around with the thin, weak soul? Am I the only one whose psyche is threadbare? Twenty-first century deities may be gaudy but they are not going to speak to us from a burning bush. For me the appeal of consumer good gods is that they stay cool; like reptiles the core temperature of most merchandise won't rise above that of their surroundings. Not that I ever heard anyone say the current deity is hot. Anyway, it is too late to recant, even in the moments when the plane might be falling off a cloud.

I'm no Saint Augustine; what I am writing is not like his *Confessions*. Augustine confessed how the ideas of the pagan philosopher Plotinus affected his mind badly. Augustine had begun to feel dirty every time he read in Plotinus's *Enneads* I.4.14, 250 CE, how it's silly "living as if man can be disengaged from the body and disdain its nominal goods." So Augustine drove himself from being lowly pagan to big boss Bishop of Hippo. I am Saint Augustine in reverse. I've gone pantheistic. Not that I mourn what has happened to Christianity since Augustine. I am more than ready for the sparkly gods and the stupid-looking gods, the flimsy gods and the family-size gods.

It turned out I didn't have the strength of character to write *The Godliness of Goods*. To do so would have required a rigorously historical methodology. Instead I surrendered to shopping cart pantheism. No, I didn't have the discipline to account for all this historically, but I can quite easily say that shopping cart pantheism is now a necessity. I just knew my dreams would confirm this, though dreams often lead to poetry, not sociology or history.

According to Aristotle, I would not have been writing history anyway because even in my fully awake state I'm too dreamy, already thinking in poetry. To legitimate how I'll carry on, here is Aristotle, from the *Poetics*:

> The historian and the poet differ not by writing in prose or in verse. The true difference is that one relates what has happened, the other what may happen. Poetry, therefore, is more philosophical than history: for poetry tends to express the universal. By the universal I mean how a person of a certain type on occasion speaks or acts according to the law of probability or necessity.[1]

Yes, I am presenting a universal, well, OK, an invitation universally seductive to North Americans: shopping cart pantheism. I can be a poet without obligation to write in verse. My poetry is more like photography than verse. My poetry is a cityscape of ideas. Yes, I have a Nikon Coolpix, though I never cared about taking competent photographs; my photos are OK as mnemonics for ideas. What can I do but stare at the mnemonics and write verselessly?

PHOTOGRAPH ONE:
"It's Nice to See You"

A magazine blurb I read on the plane described Las Vegas as "a sleepless night even during the daytime." And I had already heard the cliché that Las Vegas basically is a hallucination. My first thought upon arrival was what if I start walking along The Strip and these aren't metaphors but facts? Would I allow myself to be intimidated by facts? Years of drinking bourbon and dropping LSD had proved that in the right circumstances facts can be fabulously easy to deny. "After all," I told myself, "facts are really just poetry with the context scraped off."

I arrived at the Las Vegas airport in the middle of the night. The interior of the airport, like all the other gambling venues in Las Vegas, is adorned with a thousand points of light. Already the difference between night and day was superfluous, as was the difference between immoral and moral. As to the difference between real and fake, in Las Vegas they get to have it both ways. If you find the fake Luxor good enough (why bother travelling all the way to Egypt?), hooray for Las Vegas. If you love the absurdity of *Lago di Como* equated with a fountain "dancing" to the song "Proud to be an American," hooray for Las Vegas.

The entrance to the airport convenience store offered a long line of nested shopping carts. Printed on each handle was the phrase IT'S NICE TO SEE YOU. In the rainbow of fluorescent lights their effect was the visual equivalent of a parrot squawking "It's nice to see you. It's nice to see you. It's nice to see you. It's nice to see you. It's nice …" I hurried past the empty shopping carts and bought gum.

It has been at least 1,600 years since Gregory of Nyssa, one of the patriarchs of the early Christian church, lamented "It is not easy—in fact, it is perhaps quite impossible—to prefer the invisible good to the visible pleasant things of this life."[2] North American material plenitude has finally swollen to the point that it is completely and totally impossible to prefer the invisible good. What exactly would the invisible good include anyway? Invisible *goods* would be downright creepy. What if there are such things as invisible goods and you sense a slight buzzing sensation on your knee, what if it's an invisible electric can opener?

It is actually hard work to try forgetting all the visible goods, let alone resist ogling, desiring, touching, buying, using, displaying, storing, donating, or trashing them. Labour-saving devices were the whole point of the second half of the twentieth century. Seventy years later it takes deliberate labour to ignore the absolute excess of devices.

So many weekends are spent in shopping malls. The Shopping Channel is still extant on television. Most major merchants have a website. Fundamentalists as well as all other types of believers and nonbelievers have alleged that consumerism has already become a religion here in North America. If bad habits are all it takes to qualify as a religion, St. Paul, St. Augustine, Thomas Aquinas, and Luther wasted a lot of time and agony. St. Paul spent way more than 10,000 hours practising Christianity; as a missionary he walked 10,000 miles through Israel, Syria, Turkey, and Greece. St. Augustine composed 113 theological tomes after he converted to Christianity at age 32. On his way to Rome, St. Thomas was kidnapped by his own family. They locked him in their castle for two years. His brothers taunted him and summoned a prostitute to lure him into sin, but Thomas didn't notice. Martin Luther got struck by lightning, which turned him into a monk, a life from which he eventually recovered, and proceeded by his prodigious intellectual efforts to qualify for excommunication. If bad habits are all it takes to qualify as a religion, we North Americans are only some of the way there. We think we have forgotten God, or God has forgotten us. Not so. We have simply overlooked the holy gazillion gods that are filling up our lives.

Not that they were hoarders, but the earliest masterminds of Christianity rummaged through pagan polytheism like it was a Value Village. Ovid's *Fasti*, written in 8 CE, is a literary extravaganza about gods commemorated in the compulsory Roman festivals. For instance there was *Lemuria*. *Lemures* were souls of the dead who had not been provided decent funeral arrangements. They hated everybody and were vindictive. But they did like black beans, so you could appease them until next year if you carried a handful of black beans, tossing nine beans over your shoulder one at a time over the three days of *Lemuria*. As we all know black beans have no role in Halloween, but *lemures* do. The *Magna Maternalia* began with the felling of a pine tree. The Roman talked to the tree as if it was the goddess and adorned it with violets. The next day the chief priest cut his arms to get some blood to offer to this conifer version of the Magna Mater. Flutes, drums, and cymbals accompanied the subordinate clergy who twirled and spun and cut their arms; they also splashed the sacred pine with their blood. Long before horror films were possible, the Roman Catholic Church entertained children with stories of mutilation or murder by self or others. This sacred self-harm persists to this day in the UFC. Then there were the voluntary rites and festivities associated with Apollo, Asclepios, Bacchus, the Eleusinian Mysteries, Herakles, Hermes, Yahweh, Isis, Mithra, Orpheus, Serapis, and Zeus. There were Persian religions and Babylonian rites on offer as well.

The historians of Christianity refer discreetly to "syncretism" as the process by which this and that from all of these, and even more potently from Neo-Platonism, Gnosticism, Stoicism, and Aristotelianism, were absorbed. In other words Christianity is a mashup. The glue that finalized the *papier mâché* that is Christianity took 500 years to set. We have lived in consumerism for only 100 years. Will a few more centuries pass before consumerism gets systematized? There's nothing near a canon or dogma yet. There are millions of ads and commercials to be evaluated before such things are settled. It sounds like work. Who has the time?

The day after I arrived in Las Vegas there was an economic earthquake, the first worldwide recession of the twenty-first century. In denial of its possible long-term implications I told myself that, as did Christian martyrdom up until the fifth century CE, devastations of consumerism would inflame product pantheism even more.

PHOTOGRAPH TWO:
Travelodge Room 7

The Travelodge on The South Strip had one room available and it ameliorated my Las Vegas culture shock. The Travelodge was the only motel on The Strip unchanged since the late 1950s. The 1950s were when I was most alive without knowing it. I slept soundly and long back then. Of course I could stay awake forty-eight hours nonstop if I got enthralled by a conversation, a bus ride, or a book. Nowadays a night without slow primeval slumber will induce deliriums whether I am in hallucinogenic Las Vegas or the suburbs of Bedford.

Psychoanalytic theory will tell you that in moments of shock you regress to an earlier stage of yourself. At that point you cannot tell the difference between shock and regression. But in this motel there was no shock, no fast-forward to the unfamiliar. It was 1958 in Travelodge room 7. The clock had spines like a porcupine, the chair had legs as yellow and spindly as drinking straws, and there was a turquoise rotary dial telephone on the dresser. Twenty-first century decor would have necessitated recourse to psychoanalytic theory. Psychoanalytic theory states, "No human being is free from the strain of relating inner and outer reality."[3] Which is to say culture shock is normal. No, I got that wrong. "Sudden change, even for the better, is always a threat to the fantasy of omnipotence."[4] If I disliked anything in this room, which I didn't, I would immediately have realized I was powerless to change the decor. Omnipotence would be out of the question.

That's the principle of culture shock. Wait a minute. No, that's not right. Could it be "Sudden change, even for the better, is always a threat to the fantasy of omniscience"? In an utterly new predicament you have to face the reality that you don't have a clue what's going to happen next, or at least there's a moment of stupidity about rotary dial telephones. Know-it-all impulses peter out; gone are the delusions of limitless power. And this is what it is like to be a baby; babies' legs and arms flap around and they don't even know they have legs and arms; they can hardly do anything and what do they know? The theory is that sudden change will regress us into babies. It's only natural. Happens all the time. And when you're in a regressive state you'll believe anything. I will, if it implies I'm normal.

The Travelodge was a good change. I especially calmed down when I saw the bathroom in room 7. The bathroom became Las Vegas Photo Two. The bathroom had a pink toilet;

the toilet bowl and matching tank were a deeper pink than the seat. The shiny white lid was upright. The bathroom walls were the colour of a cocktail olive. The countertop was ochre. On the countertop stood a fresh roll of toilet paper. The brand name was *ENVISION*.

From my reading I had got the impression pagans and Christians alike were subjected to visions, especially during the first four centuries CE. The Roman Catholic Church pronounced the Roman Emperor Constantine to be a saint because of what he did decades after his vision of 312 CE. In 312 he was advancing on Rome with his army. In his own Donald-Trumpetty mind he believed he should be Emperor. There was another Roman general already in Rome who imagined himself the Emperor. On the recommendation of old-fashioned augury, this general was influenced to establish his army on the banks of the Tiber. His augurs had informed him that a sacrificial ram's liver had a wavy line inside that probably denoted a river and a sprinkle of pimples that must have symbolized his army. The message was unmistakable. On the other side of the Tiber, the night before the battle, Constantine looked up to the midnight sky and saw a ginormous shimmering cross. Or was it a ✵? Anyhow, there was also a magnificent voice reverberating from cloud to cloud. It announced, "Win with this!" The next morning Constantine ordered all his pagan soldiers to paint a Christian symbol on their shields. Constantine's army was victorious. His rival's body was found floating in the Tiber.

All that killing didn't amount to sainthood. It was because in due time after his vision, Constantine declared the Edict of Milan. The Edict decreed that Christians were tolerable. Constantine financed Christian basilicas. In 325 Constantine authorized important bishops to attend a panel discussion called the Council of Nicaea; by 325 the phenomenon of a Flesh-God entity needed an official explanation.

"Rol of Tolet Paper"

I sat on the room 7 bed to contemplate the toilet paper. The bedspread was atomic firestorm orange, a distraction I was proud to overcome. The *ENVISION* brand was entirely congruent with my growing belief in shopping cart pantheism. Grammatically speaking, the toilet paper brand name was a verb in the imperative mode just like "Win with this!" Spelling aside, "Envision!" if spoken in a loud voice would sound magisterial yet mean no more than ... —what does it mean? I couldn't decide what it meant. I only knew it was a command to product adoration.

In 1957, in a stentorian Freudian moment, the theologian Paul Tillich (1886-1965) declared that "the subconscious strivings ... determine the choice of symbols and types of faith."[5] Corporate consciousness aside, coining the brand name *ENVISION* may also, as a choice of symbol, imply a type of faith determined by unconscious strivings. *ENVISION* evokes sightings of Jesus and Mary, but only vaguely. Vague is good enough. Everyone knows that's how propaganda works. North American Jesus and Mary are pretty vague in a lot of people's Subconscious.

26
SHOPPING CART PANTHEISM

Maybe I'm not being fair, but if holy personages are that hazy, I'd say they are no more than Christian snippets. I call such snippets *christianisms*. Christianisms would be shreds of disconnected dogma. The idea of The Holy Ghost, for instance, might surface at an irrelevant moment, say rain is coming and a backlit cloud looks like a halo hovering over no one. "Ho-lee!" you might think. Christianisms are remnants of sacred similes, such as pillars of flame, an ox, and the "eyes" on a peacock's tail. What they refer to theologically is no longer an aspect of the imagery. Or you might be attracted to a colourful phrase, "Sitteth on the right hand of God" or "the whore of Babylon," that somehow sounds special. A christianism can be a free-floating word, like "multitudes" and "moneychangers." "Moneychangers" is a christianism from John 2:15-16:

> In the temple courts he [Jesus] found people selling cattle, sheep and doves, and others sitting at tables exchanging money. So he made a whip out of cords, and drove all from the temple courts, both sheep and cattle; he scattered the coins of the moneychangers and overturned their tables. To those who sold doves he said, "Get these out of here!"

A residual image of coins tumbling off upturned tables might last 2015 years. A christianism could omit the temple court buildings, or how the doves were treated, but might retain Jesus's swooping arm. Not everybody's christianisms are the same, but many are shared. Whichever nomenclature you like, snippet or christianism, these fragments are vague. Vague is not the same as forgotten. The Subconscious is elephantine that way.

A person who has rebuffed the church altogether is completely unable—as are all humans—to reject their own Subconscious, even when they suspect there's a Jesus in there. The Subconscious is not much different from the back of a tool shed; there's broken and useless stuff in there that never gets thrown out. Ideas, like objects, become mementos, and then, somehow, you can't bring yourself to chuck them. I think I am an excellent example. I know that what is left in my adult Subconscious is certainly not Christianity, but there have been christianisms in there for decades. Christianisms are the slivers stuck in my own flabby soul, a soul that was graceless to begin with. I had no skill at Christianity. I suited up on Sundays but I knew I was useless to the team. Now I'm signed with the idols.

Christianisms, however, are as powerful as Christianity. Broken glass is jagged. I was just guessing that the Christian splinters in my brain are typical; the details were indistinct until I walked around Las Vegas.

PHOTOGRAPH THREE:
The Miracle Mile

With early Christian history in mind, I stepped out the door and into the Travelodge parking lot. I felt like I was stepping into the Roman Coliseum. I even justified the feeling. The parking lot was vast. The few cars parked there were really big. All their hungry grills were facing me. I raised my eyes to the heavens. The cloudless sky was royal blue and infinite. Above and beyond the cars I could see all the way to the Eiffel Tower. The retinal effect of the extreme blue background was to outline every strut of the Tower latticework in hot pink as if the Tower was wearing a see-through negligée. Instantly, I was reliving the ten seconds I had spent in the Toronto airport's full-torso security scanner. Finally, naughty boys have achieved x-ray vision, and they didn't even have to wear nerdy spectacles to see through my clothes. Exposed, my reflex had been to modestly lower my eyes.

Now I was lowering my eyes again, as if I was the one with x-ray vision, as if I was embarrassing the Eiffel Tower, peeping at her from a parking lot. Eyes lowered, I was in fact staring straight at a huge white wall about half a block away. The wall was five storeys high and ten storeys long. Nailed to an enormous blood-red rectangle were the pure white words **MIRACLE MILE**. Was that how far Jesus lugged the cross to Golgotha? I couldn't remember. Maybe the miracle was that a made-in-the-USA Eiffel Tower was exactly a mile from the sign. That didn't matter either. I rejoiced that an instance of commodity adoration was right there in the picture. And a psychoanalyst couldn't possibly complain that I wasn't seeing it right. The Freudian formula is, take a phenomenon like Jesus withering a fig tree to prove a point; reduce the story to one little thing, say the printed word *Miracle*; slap the one little thing onto something else entirely, a 100,000-square-foot shopping centre, for instance. This is a perfect example of neurotic thinking—condensation (instead of a tale, just one word) and displacement (*Miracle* isn't printed on the original withered fig tree in Jerusalem; it's printed on a building in Las Vegas).

If this Las Vegas Miracle Mile is a symptom of neurotic anxiety, what caused it? Where and when and why did this neurotic anxiety erupt? How could such a neurosis have been so irrepressible, so pervasive, that it changed our North American way of life?

For another example, could anyone miss what an apple with one bite taken out of it alludes to? This computer logo has got to be ironic, as well as grandiose, and a theological challenge too. The logo implies "One sample and your life will never be the same (You remember what happened to Adam and Eve, ha ha)." And its grandiosity touts, "Our product is so powerful (like Jehovah is or The Serpent was, or both) it has changed the pace of business. And your domestic life too, everywhere, forever." And maybe it was in fact chosen as a spiritual challenge, "Yeah, a chewed apple used to refer to Genesis, but our product is bigger than the Bible." How can it not refer to the most famous "apple" in Judeo-Christian history, the one that ruined everything? For their logo the company could just as well have chosen a box with an open lid, Pandora's box, a pagan legend. Pagan, Christian, a fairy tale is a fairy tale. Were those design freaks at Apple really thinking no further than a fruit (with a play on the *Macintosh* company name)? Is their product branded with a symbol for the Fall of Mankind? At Apple Inc. the echo of a Biblical allusion may be no louder than a worm's heartbeat.

I had read a lot about miracles. For all of its 1,000 years, the Roman Empire was hell on earth. This would have included the Christianizing era between zero and 400 CE. People needed a lot more miracles than they got. It was a hideous life for plebeians, soldiers, and slaves. Everywhere you turned somebody was mutilated or dying a morbidly gruesome death. Necrotizing fasciitis ruled. Miracles, however, are a matter of context. If one of my precious family members' lives was saved in a four-billion dollar hospital with a staff numbering the population of Kalamazoo, Michigan, with a team of sixteen surgeons and sixteen nurses removing a tiny brain polyp, and nothing bad ever happening to that precious family member ever again, I'd call that a miracle. You know Jesus wouldn't have said "Yeah, but could they do it in less than one second?" If he even thought such a thing Jesus would have been referring to a miracle seemingly performed by only one person, himself. Jesus would have been referring to his own thirty-seven instantaneous miracles. He did turn water into wine, walk on water he hadn't turned into wine, and find a coin in a fish's mouth, along with exorcisms and raising the dead. We are grateful to have a four-billion dollar hospital with all those trained health care providers, but isn't that the way it should be? Most hospitals in North America are saving one life an hour minimum, one miracle an hour in New Testament terms. Occasionally, it is broadcast and actually named as a miracle when an infant from some bleak outpost gets unprecedented surgery in a big city hospital. Is it because the infant is so tiny and the hospital so large that the surgery is recognized as the miracle it really is?

In other arenas of North American prowess, "miracle" was also not applied to achievements that were actually prodigious. Even during FDR's socialist programs, a stupendous feat wasn't ballyhooed as a blue-collar miracle. The Hoover Dam was compared to the pagan pyramids. It certainly was not likened to the colossal job done by Gregory the Wonder-Worker who in 240 CE changed the course of a river in Turkey.

The *What's Cooking* website informs us

> First introduced at the 1933 Century of Progress Chicago World's Fair, *Kraft Miracle Whip* soon launched one of the biggest food advertising campaigns to ever grace the U.S. media—from print to TV. And this initial effort led to 22 weeks of almost non-stop advertising, including a weekly two-hour radio show.

The use of the word "whip" does not allude to the John 2:15-16 report of Jesus's outburst in the Temple courts. Apparently, it refers to the action of the machine that coagulates soybean oil, sugar, vinegar, undisclosed spices, egg, and air into a salad dressing. The Kraft technicians were understandably proud of their machine, which might account for the salad dressing's exuberant label. Perhaps the real miracle is that no one in the advertising department realized they had just devised a brand name for an automated S&M sex toy.

PHOTOGRAPH FOUR:
The Eternal City

Two in the afternoon in the desert is the time for lethal heat strokes. Poetry and my Death Instinct propelled me: I went for a walk. Not that my Death Instinct could possibly be fulfilled with so many air-conditioned buildings to escape into. When I am sure I have the upper hand, unlike in an airplane, arousing the Death Instinct enhances my image as a devil-may-care type. In severe Freudian psychoanalytic terms, you can't deliberately have a relationship with your Death Instinct for very long. And even if you think you are at one with your Death Instinct, it is ultimately just another concept; it is not a way of life. Freud claimed that all living things have an irresistible and innate tendency to return to a mere element, like boron, molybdenum, or tin. Freud never could have imagined couch potatoes. Freud never mentioned laziness, but it is a feeble version of the Death Instinct: that moment when instead of changing the kitty litter you sigh, change your mind, and sit back down. Freud insisted that the endpoint of the human Death Instinct is ultimate laziness: a spineless mineral. Something within us is compelling us to lapse into the senseless desiccated state of ore. Walking on hot coals, in other words a Las Vegas sidewalk, I felt cocky enough to bluff my Death Instinct, "What can you do with this, eh? Eh?"

I walked through the alley in the shadow of the Travelodge office at my right and a boarded-up SNAK shop along the left. The outside wall of the Travelodge office was lake-blue painted upon which glacial-white letters spelled GRAB-N-GO BEVERAGES 10¢. I went inside and bought a cold Dr. Pepper for USD$2.25. It quenched my Death Instinct and I resumed walking down the alley. In fifteen seconds I was at the intersection of the alley and South Strip Boulevard.

I am compelled to turn left rather than right whenever pragmatism is irrelevant. I must always remind myself that political consciousness is more than casting a vote. I turned left. Heat from the abrasive sun had excoriated the pavement. My sneakers were already filling with steam. As a distraction from my sneakers I looked up to the parched sign above me, COLD BEER TATTOO. The sign was almost as tall as the little wooden shop beneath it. I noticed the shopkeeper. He was standing by a beach-towel Elvis image as washed out as the Shroud of Turin.

Nobody wanted Elvis to die ever. Among his devotees are the thousands who know he never did die. Alternatively, a devotee could have harboured the unholy suspicion that Elvis was the Egyptian Osiris. If so Elvis would certainly not have to stay dead. The consequence, however, would be imagining the part of the legend where Elvis/Osiris gets chopped into twenty-four pieces; then, every one of them is gathered up and glommed back together except for his penis. Unlike Jesus, whose sightings are infrequent, you might spot Elvis anywhere anytime. I myself saw him the summer of 1991. He was at the wheel of a brown 1980 Chevy pickup taking US 78 West into Tupelo.

It's respectful that Elvis icons and amulets are mass-marketed in every form known to Christian civilization. On The South Strip I had wanted to find an Elvis locket; maybe it would be pinned inside one of those greeting cards that opens to play a tinny little tune. The card would bleat Elvis's very own composition "Miracle of the Rosary," performed in Arkansas in 1957.

The COLD BEER TATTOO shopkeeper's face was also excoriated, sandblasted by the desert winds. He was drier than jerky. His expression was so numb that boredom probably would have thrilled him. I never would have photographed him. I never willingly take photos of people. There's something about taking pictures of people that gives me the creeps. It is true that many things give me the creeps. I claim it's Existential awareness. There's a mean little Jean-Paul Sartre in my Super-Ego.

> In all the actions a man may take in order to create himself as he wills himself to be, there is not one that is not, at the same time, creating an image of Man as we believe he ought to be.[6]

So, if I photograph people, I observe them according to political, aesthetic, and social values I freely create. If I photographed people, I would not be making a record of how they want to communicate themselves to me. I would be photographing them for the sole purpose of exhibiting my very own chosen beliefs. The camera would be exploiting the light reflected from a person's body, perhaps even the light reflected from their soul … Just kidding! The light reflected from a person's body, as from any object, would provide the camera with a design. Certainly the camera is capable of intelligent design, but for argument's sake maybe the person whose light rays the camera manipulates happens to prefer another kind of design. Too bad, because I am "creating an image of Man as we believe he ought to be," which has nothing to do with the model's liberty to chose. Sure the model can chose to misbehave, but are we literally talking about photography, or the processes that impel it? Commandeering someone's reflected light as if they are readily available in a mineral state would be no different than taking that photograph of the Travelodge bathroom. How could I do something like that with my camera? How could such a portrait bring goodness into the world if it is inherently a result of subjugation? Why would I want the whole world to do as I do? What kind of "Man as we believe he ought to be" is that? As soon as the shopkeeper disappeared into the dark shadows of his store, I pulled out my Coolpix.

Under the COLD BEER TATTOO sign dangled an older smaller one, CITY TATTOO. The colours once were orange, green, yellow, and black. This sign boasted that the tattoos were **FREEHAND BY ARTISTS TAKES FIVE MINUTES STAYS ON**. Next I noticed some orange, green, yellow, and black raincoats that looked like they had also been dangling on the shop, entrance ceiling since 1962, the last time it rained. In the distance behind the wooden shop, two mammoth hotels stretched into the stratosphere. The bald white one looked to be 1970s style. The unfinished blue one towering beside it appeared to be sprouting little post-modern wings. In parental stance two gangly red cranes stood close by ready to hoist. Realigning my gaze to the foreground, I saw the one detail that revealed how the rickety shop has stayed in business all these decades: the array of fresh white **YES WE CAN** T-shirts. I wondered whether if I had gone way to the back inside I would have found **ICH BIN EIN BERLINER** ones.

The entire vista was a twenty-first century version of Freud's picture of the Subconscious.

> ... In mental life nothing which has been once formed can perish ... everything is somehow preserved and ... in suitable circumstances (when, for instance, regression goes back far enough) it can once more be brought to light. Let us try to grasp what this assumption involves by taking an analogy from another field. We will choose as an example the history of the Eternal City ...

> ... Let us, by a flight of imagination, suppose that Rome is not a human habitation but a psychical entity with a similarly long and copious past—an entity, that is to say, in which nothing that has once come into existence will have passed away and all the earlier phases of development continue to exist alongside the latest one. This would mean that in Rome the palaces of the Caesars and the Septizonium of Septimius Severus would still be rising to their old height on the Palatine and that the castle of S. Angelo would still be carrying on its battlements the beautiful statues which graced it until the siege by the Goths, and so on... Where the Coliseum now stands we could at the same time admire Nero's vanished Golden House ... indeed, the same piece of ground would be supporting the church of Santa Maria sopra Minerva and the ancient temple over which it was built.[7]

After Constantine many Christian Emperors sanctioned urban and spiritual renewal through arson and the looting of traditional pagan shrines. Eventually, the popes would also join in. It became virtuous to recycle and reuse marble and fine wood from demolished temples to build Christian basilicas. The original temple of Isis, for example, must have looked like a landfill site after the Emperor Zacharias wrecked it to pave the way for Santa Maria sopra Minerva.

> Most sacred Emperors! Strip the temples of their ornaments, strip and fear not. Let those vain gods be melted down by the fire of the mint or the blaze of the metal-worker's flame.

> Transfer all the temple gifts to the use of yourselves and of the Lord. Since you destroyed the temples, you have advanced mightily by the strong help of God.[8]

"Dagon"

The artists who adorned the new churches with Jesus stories couldn't, no more than they can now, invent blessed imagery *ex nihilo*. The Holy Ghost was never promoted to Muse. The portrayals of Mary, the baby Jesus, the disciples, apostles, the Holy Ghost itself, and as time went on the saints, would look as remarkably familiar to fourth century churchgoers as when the churchgoers had been pagans. New converts would feel right at home with sequels to the Dionysian Mysteries, Mithraism, or Babylonian rites.

Establishing a look is a matter of very artful tweaking. The similarities between papal mitres and the hat of Dagon the Mesopotamian fish god are reminders that fashion crimes are as old as humanity itself. The white crown of the Upper Egypt pharaoh is often cited to prove papal haberdashers were copycats.

Dr. Pepper induced an unprecedented lucidity, not because I hadn't drunk one before and not because I'd never drunk one under the influence of 104 degrees Fahrenheit. I had spent my childhood at the same temperature, suffused with this same faux prune refreshment. The difference is that now I can read French. A paragraph from Bréhier's 1927 article in *Revue Philosophique* bubbled up. Suddenly Bréhier was fizzing through the Freudian metaphor of The Eternal City. Freud's metaphor began to quake with promise. I swirled back into the alley. I paddled through the heat waves as fast as I could. I held my breath till I got back to room 7. My handwritten copy of Bréhier's supposition was in my notebook somewhere. Was it caffeine and sugar or intellectual exhilaration that shook my fingers? I made a sloppy translation as I reread:

> The Cosmos of the Greeks is a world, in effect, without history, an interminable Order that cannot be excoriated by time, an Order that stays exactly like itself forever such that events always end up where they started, and therefore cyclical changes repeat themselves ad infinitum. The inverse idea, that there could be a radical change in reality, a wholesale intrusion by a new truth—this would utterly unhinge the Hellenic universe. (Paris: Librairie Félix Alcan) page 8.

I try not to notice when current events begin to repeat themselves. I'll go into denial if I have to. Historians no doubt could immediately console me that, for instance, North American democracy doesn't stay exactly like itself forever such that events always end up where they started, cyclical changes repeating themselves ad infinitum. That's the little picture. Sure, people run for office on promises and when they get elected they don't fulfill them. Either they get voted in the next time around or they don't; yet someone gets voted in on promises. But this is not at all the same as the ancient Greek cosmology. Maybe what it's really about is guaranteed satisfaction just to hear someone even make a promise. It isn't about promises being broken. Like everyone else I am too ill-informed to recognize change that actually hadn't been promised. Obviously, my fascination with promises is politically extraneous. My preoccupation with promises must be a symptom of a post-crucifixion *christianism*. A New Era, a historical rupture, is always supposed to be coming our way. First we got a once-in-a-lifetime uniquely unnatural biological discontinuity: offspring conceived by the Holy Ghost, born of the Virgin. Then we get another once-in-a-lifetime uniquely unnatural biological discontinuity: rising live from a tomb. Next, time is supposed to develop a rupture when past and present are simultaneous in the future: "He shall come to judge the living and the dead."

I suspect that ruptures will always seem normal in my Subconscious, even if now they are always trivial. In 500 BCE would our routine twenty-first century commercials have seemed a wholesale intrusion of a new truth? Would "alviarmani.com award-winning, A NEW ERA IN HAIR TRANSPLANTS!" unhinge the Hellenic universe?

My shopping cart pantheism, I exclaimed to myself, had not been the simple result of a digestive process. In my Subconscious Jesus had been like an absentee landlord neglecting all the vacant Christian premises. Consumerism wasn't like Revelation evicting Dialectic, or Haussmann renovating Paris. Compared to the Hellenic psyche my christianistic post-post-modern North American Subconscious was a condemned building. Like squatters, merchandise deities had just moved right in.

PHOTOGRAPH FIVE:
Hells

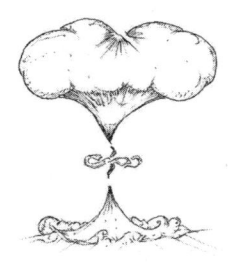

"Mushroom Cloud"

Between 1900 and 1968 (year of the Nuclear Non-Proliferation Treaty), North American people were beset by too many man-made/woman-complicit disasters: first, the invention of the automobile and airplane enabled addiction to oil and speed. Then came mechanization of slaughter in World War I. Next the Great Depression. Then Nazi ideology and the Holocaust. World War II had to happen. The Atom Bomb was dropped on Hiroshima and Nagasaki. Consciousness kept rising toward nuclear annihilation. In 1959 Ruth Nanda Anshen, one of many brooding sociologists, observed, "the present apocalyptic period is one of exceptional tensions."[9] Every psyche in North America was experiencing exceptional tension. One after another these apocalypses had detonated in every North American psyche. Psychoanalysts should probably have looked for mass regression, given one culture shock after another, one apocalypse after another. Yet not one of them saw it. Not one of them posited the syndrome "Post-Apocalyptic Regression." So I made it up just now. "Apocalypsis" would also be a suitable term.

Post-apocalyptic regression was a kind of brain damage. The cortical grey matter rolled up like a frayed carpet. Fantasies of omnipotence were mistaken for hope. Fantasies of omniscience were mistaken for science. Reductivism replaced interpretation.

Post-apocalyptic cognitive changes in the general populace resulted in all TV commercials seeming realistic. When commercials reduced everything to The Thing to have or to do, they made sense literally, which is the only sense to make when your mind is in tatters from too many apocalypses. Millions of brains succumbed to post-apocalyptic regression. "The human body" began to make sense as just another thing based on input and output. La Mettrie had insisted upon such during the Enlightenment, but after the massive effects of science gone mad between 1914 and 1945, scientism became an ideology:

> The thing I like about my body is that it's strong.... It's a well functioning machine.[10]

The result was that only blatant gratification was comprehensible. Man as machine could have provoked a return to Puritanism: Keep the machine clean. Don't wear it out. You'll be paying for it many years to come. But that didn't happen.

Self-denial hurts. The apocalypses had hurt too much already. Internal combustion machines provided the best expression for every apocalypsis sufferer: "Fill 'er up." It was the reverse of the Enlightenment. Facts and objects seemed so sturdy; dialectical inquiry became icky. Debate became a formality. Evidence devolved into a Perry Mason TV-plot gimmick.

Or could one explain this post-apocalyptic syndrome as *en masse* regression to Egypt, 1945 BCE?

> He [the Egyptian] had a concrete mind. He wanted his gods to assume a recognizable shape. Why then should he not worship a beetle ... the Egyptian believed in a fluid life force that could be poured at will into any suitable mold.... The life spirit was protean: it transformed itself effortlessly into a multiplicity of shapes.[11]

According to shopping cart pantheism, insects wouldn't qualify to join diamond rings, smartphones, or gel shoe inserts in the twenty-first century pantheon. Twenty-first century pantheism excludes anything the ancients or my contemporaries would consider Natural. By "Natural," I refer to something, even if inanimate, that remains in the environment where it developed. Rocks and stones seem inherently placid and unresponsive stuck in their surroundings, but rocks and stones actually cannot be trusted. They have been integral to the planet since pre-hominid times. They have been worshipped. They have a reputation for success in magic activities. How do we know rocks are lying around without plans? The Natural World is creepy;

"A cupcake"

to contemplate all that pullulating, fertilizing, and symbioting is not only unnerving, it's exhausting. Shopping cart pantheism doesn't deal with these worries. Actually, shopping cart pantheism doesn't deal with anything. But Natural objects don't fit in. A bamboo forest is Natural. A bamboo shoot is Natural. You can stick a bamboo chopstick in the shopping cart pantheon. Those adorable macaque monkeys leaping onto everything and everybody in Gibraltar are as Natural as you can get. Subject one of them to a taxidermy job and it becomes a divinity. A seashell that stays where it washed up is Natural. Take it to your souvenir shop, paint it with clear nail polish, put a $1 sticker on it and it's ready for the pantheon.

As I was born in 1943, obviously apocalypsis accounts for my own severe case of shopping cart pantheism. It is for readers to decide, however, whether my capacity for heuristic analysis, dialectic argument, and abstract thinking have been injured by post-apocalyptic regression.

In 1945, by the time WWII had ended, church congregations must have seemed to be either daydreaming or stupefied. Disquieted by this, the great modern Christian theologians got overheated as if it was 1545 all over again when Martin Luther had begged "to become kneaded into one cake with God (*mit Gott ein Kuche werden*)."[12] Unfortunately, mid-century theologians' grasp of reality was not comforting. Their exhortations became extreme, their language too abstract. As executive chefs, the theologians weren't serving sweet metaphors, and they gave the impression Jesus wanted everything for himself:

> Jesus' demands arise out of the knowledge that one cannot fulfill the will of God up to a certain point, but rather that God demands the whole man.[13]
>
> God creates out of nothing, and whoever becomes nothing before him is made alive.[14]

Then Tillich started emphasizing that true Christian faith "unites all elements of man's personal life, the bodily, the unconscious, the conscious, the spiritual.... In the act of faith every nerve of man's body, every striving of man's soul, every function of man's spirit participates."[15] On top of all the conscious moral pressures of the past 1,950 years, Christians were now directed to get self-conscious about their Subconscious.

PHOTOGRAPH SIX:
Twentieth Century Rabid Skunk

Freud, whether he knew it consciously or not, assumed that the human psyche is a system, a system like hydraulics:

> Force that is applied at one point is transmitted to another point using an incompressible fluid. The fluid is almost always an oil of some sort.[16]

In spite of the sincerest efforts of the Super-Ego, the pressure of Id-oil will sometimes push a human Ego to behave like a rabid skunk.

The rabid skunk's name was Edward Bernays (1891-1995). He promoted himself as "The Father of Public Relations." He claimed credit for conjuring most of the methods businesses and governments have used to hypnotize the public since the beginning of the twentieth century. Freud's sister was the mother of Edward Bernays. Edward Bernays's father was the brother of Freud's wife. Throughout the 1920s and 1930s, although Freud and Bernays's relationship included numerous conversations, Bernays was not his uncle's acolyte. To Bernays there was no consanguinity between human suffering and psychoanalytic theory; the connection between the two was a coincidence. Freudian psychoanalytic theory was to Bernays a gadget, a fabulously advantageous gadget. The scientism of the Freudian quest and the glamour of technology came to a boil in Bernays's hype thirsty mind. His publicity schemes signalled a qualitative change in the relations between powerful groups and ordinary citizens. This change, *modernization,* was aggressively secular.

Bernays's clients included General Electric, General Motors, Procter & Gamble, Nash-Kelvinator, Philco Radio and Television, U.S. Radium, the New York Philharmonic Orchestra, playwright Eugene O'Neill, dancer Nijinsky, singer extraordinaire Enrico Caruso, and painter Georgia O'Keeffe, as well as Mutual Benefit Life Insurance, Title Guarantee and Trust, Columbia Broadcasting System, National Broadcasting Company, *Cosmopolitan*, *Fortune*, *Good Housekeeping*, *Ladies' Home Journal*, *The New Republic* and *Time* magazines, A&P, F. W. Woolworth, R. H. Macy, and Mack Trucks. Bernays was also the public relations counsel for United Fruit Company, who benefited when Bernays inflamed public denunciation of Guatemala's socialist president, Jacobo Árbenz Guzmán.

Freudian psychoanalysis was philosophically modern (prizing reason above tradition). More significantly it presented consciousness as accessible to objective study. This objective study was based on the duality of subject and object. Freudianism presented psyche as *thing* to be analyzed. Freudianism made psyche seem an adjustable system, not an existentially shared predicament. By presenting a subjective psyche as an object of scrutiny, by emphasizing how consciousness functions like a mechanism, the structure of Freudian dualism was inherently technological. A technology of the psyche is the technology of a system; it is not comprehension of shared humanly being. Based on a Freudian duality of subject and object, public relations was definitely a technology, a technology for regulating the susceptible individual's (the customer's, the citizen's) inclination.

The explanation Bernays gave for public relations was that the psyche system succumbs very readily to "the appeal of indirection." In spite of overt theatricality, the effects of public relations were insidious. Bernays had a sneaky mind. The assumption is that the system called psyche is driven by intimate, even preverbal forces. Handily for public relations, these forces normally attach to memories. For a client company's ad Bernays would select images most likely to evoke a vivid affirmative memory, and Presto!, unleash the hydraulic psychical force. When the force was unleashed it was diverted to the company product. This amounts to employing the mechanism of neurosis—condensation and displacement—in the service of selling products.

At first, in 1923, Bernays described this public relations activity as "crystallizing public opinion," but by 1947 he said it was "engineering consent."

> "The conscious and intelligent manipulation of the organized habits and opinions of the masses is an important element in democratic society," Bernays wrote in his 1928 book *Propaganda*. "Those who manipulate this unseen mechanism of society constitute an invisible government which is the true ruling power of our country."[17]

If you're still thinking in old-fashioned Judeo-Christian ways, your uneasiness would be whether this manipulation is for good or for evil. If you're even more old-fashioned and thinking like a sixth century BCE sophist, the concern would be whether or not the citizenry will succumb to the rhetoric.

Bernays still had clients in 1991; he had lived to age 103. Many more than a mere twelve men on Madison Avenue became Bernays's disciples.

PHOTOGRAPH SEVEN:
Dogmatics in Outline

Years before the Las Vegas pilgrimage, my list of midcentury celebrity theologians was already long enough. Exemplary among them was Karl Barth, a walking talking monument to the *Doxa*. The only work of Karl Barth that I bothered to read was the 1949 Philosophical Library, Inc. translation of *Dogmatics in Outline*. Barth had lectured, as he described, "in the semi-ruins of the once stately Kurfürsten Schloss"[18] in Bonn in 1947. He had ad libbed for the first time ever, so the *Outline* was revamped from a transcript written in shorthand.

Barth had refused to sign an oath of allegiance to Hitler. And Barth was one of the God-fearing ringleaders of the 1934 Barmen Declaration that rebuked the Christian churches of

Germany who were comfy with National Socialism. Barth was fortunate enough to be banished by the Nazis. Banishment was good, considering the alternatives. But Barth was a citizen of Switzerland, a country the Nazis would not have wanted to annoy. I've seen many a photograph of theologians on the covers of their books, and Barth is the only one who is giggling.

Barth wasn't particularly known to the North American general public until a few years before his death in 1968. Barth had got famous exaggerating how almighty the Lord was, how the Lord was incomprehensibly beyond human consciousness. By 1962 Karl Barth's stunning commentary *The Epistle to the Romans* had been in print for forty years. His *Kirchliche Dogmatik* (said to be six million words long) was still unfinished, but this too he had begun to write three decades earlier. By 1962, after half a century of global apocalypses, including the postwar onslaught by the advertising industry, Barth might have been the only theologian in Christendom who wasn't shell-shocked. Robert Vickrey's portrait of Barth, painted for the 1962 cover of *TIME* magazine, however, depicted Barth scowling like the jealous Yahweh. Barth's portrait may have been intended to challenge the power of The Bomb itself. It could very well have conveyed to all the miserable magazine readers that Barth considered them lowlier than the citizens of Asdod:

> There was a deadly destruction throughout all the city; the hand of God was very heavy there. And the men that died not were smitten with the emerods [hemorrhoids].[19]

Or was it that Barth must appear gravely strained due to the superhuman energy it takes to think? Most magazine subscribers fancy and plain hadn't been protected from WWII heartache any better than blasphemers, atheists, and heathens. The Holocaust had proved the Reformation was crap. A theologian, even Karl Barth, on the cover of *TIME* looked like emotional blackmail. It would have been relevant and necessary to have depicted Barth smiling through his tears—but he wasn't; to commission a merciless frown betrayed the editors' post-apocalyptic regression had gone back to 1962 BCE, when Yahweh blamed his victims.

Dogmatics in Outline is the kind of used book I buy on impulse. Judging books by their cover is like a Kinder Egg experience. *Outline* has a wan blue dust jacket exactly matching my wan blue soul. Otherwise the cover design is barren, displaying only the title in extra skinny Palatino Linotype. This hardcover edition is elegantly thin, and so I had assumed it was in a class with Freud's *Civilization and its Discontents*, Descartes's *Meditations on First Philosophy*, and Kant's *Prolegomena to any Future Metaphysics*, each one splendid in 30,000 words or less.

I read the *Outline* twice. In the *Outline* Barth storms through The Apostles' Creed. For a mere flotsam of Creed I had to weather a deluge of Barth's rhetoric. I nearly drowned in a catechismal flash flood. By 1962 it had been too late to look anywhere but to advertising for such blatant exaggeration. To the '60s generation, Barth's gusto for the oldie but goodie God would have sounded like amateur ad copy. Fortunately, I always read between the lines. That's where consumer pantheism usually seeps right in.

I'd flipped room 7's bedspread on its back. The underside was frizzy pale grey, like winter snow that piles in gutters. The air conditioner was bawling like the North Wind and felt like it. A thick white sheet of plastic blocked the tiny back window, making the room look like it was crammed against an iceberg. The chill was miserable, for which I was grateful. Anything to distract from reviewing my Barth notes. The best way to review ideas anyway is to watch a hockey game on television. Room 7 didn't have a television. You're supposed to go out and watch Las Vegas.

"Blow Dryer."

I opened the door. The evening air was like a blow-dryer. I didn't walk far. I stood at the corner of Las Vegas Boulevard and Tropicana Avenue. Thousands of people in shorts and T-shirts were streaming along The Strip. Many of them carried jumbo pink, green, or purple drinks. Many of them had pink, green, or purple dribbles on their necks. No one seemed giddy yet no one seemed pressed. We were like a school of fish, and all with that same guppy stare. *Sanctorum communionem*, The Righteous Crowd, that's us. Who else is there? Who else has there ever been? It's humans or nobody. We're all that the late Father Almighty ever had.

In 1969, Benedict XVI himself, when he was living under the name Ratzinger, had nudged souls toward product adoration. I'm not claiming he knew what he was doing, but he specifically said, "… the word *sanctorum* ('of the holy ones') does not refer

58
SHOPPING CART PANTHEISM

to persons but means the holy *thing*."[20] He didn't explain how *sanctorum* got from plural to singular. To me this grammatical parapraxis revealed a footstep toward the twenty-first century. Obviously, Ratzinger had not noticed the drastic implications of a holy *thing*.

PHOTOGRAPH EIGHT:
The King

I was walking by the open foyer of a bar above which spasmodic red lights spelled //-// TRANCE //-// //-// ENTRANCE //-// TRANCE //-// //-// ENTRANCE. In the glare I thought I saw The King. The big fellow was leaning on a tall spindly table shaped like a martini glass. His head was angled out of view behind an inflatable eight-foot tall, four-foot diameter plastic Budweiser bottle. His right leg was gently crossed past his left leg, displaying the flare of the bell-bottoms and the glossy white height of his high-heeled boots. He was wearing a white jumpsuit with an upturned collar. The suit top was unbuttoned down to the hefty gold belt buckle. He wasn't wearing an undershirt. The jumpsuit was hauling I'd say forty pounds of rhinestone. I was agog. His was the most relaxed posture I'd ever seen in my life. Upon which vision that cheerless Jean-Paul Sartre entity in my brain started nagging about bad faith:

> All his behaviour seems to us a game. He applies himself to chaining his movements as if they were mechanisms, the one regulating the other; his gestures and even his voice seem to be mechanisms.... He is playing, he is amusing himself. But what is he playing? We need not watch long before we can explain it: he is playing at being [The King] ... in a cafe. There is nothing there to surprise us. The game is a kind of marking out and investigation.... In the cafe [he] plays with his condition in order to realize it. This obligation is not different from that which is imposed on all tradesmen. Their condition is wholly one of ceremony. The public demands of them that they realize it as a ceremony.[21]

The public demands of them that they realize they are commodities, as Karl Marx had lamented. "A product," as team managers refer to hockey players at the trade deadline. Sartre whether he knew it or not was equating play with ceremony. For hockey this is accurate. A hockey game is a sacred ritual. Some psychoanalysts claim ceremony and play "are where living is at its most intense."[22] Tell that to a French resistance fighter or a victim of the Abu Ghraib torture cells—Sartre would have said these are where life is at its most intense. Would Barth have agreed with the psychoanalysts? He still had some giggle left in him after the war.

PHOTOGRAPH NINE:
My Hanky

After about an hour in room 7, I was eager for some sunburn. This time I turned to the right at Las Vegas Boulevard. I believed I was strolling along The Miracle Mile. Not so. The Miracle Mile is the length of a mall perpendicular to Las Vegas Boulevard. The doors of the mall open at the same angle as Rio de Janeiro's *Cristo Redentor*. Then the doors close. It's automatic. The doors opened again. The doors flapped peacefully like the wings of a snow-white dove. The Miracle Mile was exhaling an air-conditioned πνεύμα, the breath that is the soul itself. My lungs fell into rhythm with the huge unhurried doors. I paused agape. I shivered. It was the air-conditioning, not something supernatural. I do know *agape* in Greek means "what God prefers." *Agape* cannot possibly apply to doors. Doors don't

"A Pair of White Socks"

prefer anything. That's why you will find them in the product pantheon.

I reached into my front pocket for my handkerchief. The pocket was empty. If I should ever lose my hanky, death drowning in sweat would be a blessing. I cannot lose my hanky. I cannot. I will not. The hanky is an exquisite product, light, white, and without a will of its own. It is divine.

I got back to room 7 fast. I didn't remember packing my hanky as if it was an article of clothing. Could it possibly be in my little green duffle bag? I flung everything out of the bag: a pair of black cotton shorts, two more white cotton T-shirts, two more white cotton undershirts, two more pairs of white cotton socks, two more pairs of white cotton underwear, six hardcover books. There was a kind of blasphemy to the frenzy of all that tossing. I felt witless. I felt fear. I felt queasy. I was afraid to look in the mirror; my face might be uncanny. I was staring at the desktop, yet why would the hanky be there?

Near a purple metal ashtray lay a white paper cocktail napkin. A little red silhouette profile was printed on it. **CAESARS PALACE** was printed underneath it, with LAS VEGAS printed under that. Its presence taunted me. It was like a demonic reversal.

My hanky is only a thing. The hanky is a thing and nothing more. These are the facts of it: it was an unsought gift that has stayed with me for thirty years. The hanky is not transcendent. It is tangible. I could pinch myself up one side and down another;

64
SHOPPING CART PANTHEISM

this would merely demonstrate that I am not the same kind of tangible as an inanimate hanky. An inherently lifeless product is ineffably different from human consciousness. In fact that's how Barth had described God. Ancient Greek philosophers surmised that "God is called Artificer and ... part of him extends through everything"[23] "present in all men, though they are unaware of it."[24] We humans manufacture, we are artificers, but nothing we construct is imbued with what we are. As a poet, maybe someday I'll write about our productions as our mirrors. But we do know that even moving reflections in mirrors are inanimate material and similes are always insightful.

My hanky satisfies Gregory of Nyssa's recipe for a God: "simple, uniform and noncomposite."[25] My hanky is simple. It has no articulated parts. It is definitely noncomposite: it is substance only, no soul, no élan, no anima, no spirit, no metaphysical anything.

We can credit inanimate purchases with any fantasy or fact we wish, they will not acknowledge it. But it's a lot easier to just not imbue them with anything. That's what is so convenient. What you think, feel, or imagine to be embodied by consumer goods doesn't affect them. They don't care because they cannot care. We can relax and take our fantasies elsewhere.

How great it would feel to produce a life form *de novo*. Many people are working on this, but it hasn't happened yet. And when it does, those life forms might realize, as do I, that the product deities are wondrously and definitely unlike us life forms. Every marvellously insensate product is not only without life, it is without death. That impresses me. Only the living must die. How can anyone refuse such absolute otherness a niche in the pantheon? That's exactly what the ancient Greeks decided 3,000 years ago. They called their gods The Immortals. Then they luridly embellished them. That's what advertising does to our consumable immortals: the same storylines, artlessly tweaked to avoid offending anyone. I rummaged in all my pants pockets again. The hanky was in the left front pocket!

Apparently, until she handed it to me, the hanky had been in my grandmother's possession since the late 1930s. The hanky is white linen. *Linda*, in a sweet blue script, is centred over one corner and finished within a simple blue scalloped medallion. The fine blue hems were rolled by hand. There has never been anyone in our family named Linda.

Now I was free to concede I quite liked the Caesars Palace paper napkin. I pressed it between pages of Rudolf Otto's *The Idea of the Holy*.

PHOTOGRAPH TEN:
Advertese

By the beginning of the twentieth-first century, we were all fluent in advertese. The cover of O THE OPRAH MAGAZINE met industry hype standards in October 2010 with LIVE YOUR BEST LIFE, UNLOCK YOUR INNER SUPERSTAR, THE O-POWER LIST! 20 WOMEN WHO ARE ROCKING THE WORLD, SPECIAL URGENT MESSAGE FROM DR. OZ, THE PERFECT $49 FALL SHOE. Whether Oprah knew it or not, if you say "fall shoe" over and over again faster and faster, it will sound like "false you." Oprah couldn't have known it; is it the sniffle of a christianism in her guilty Subconscious? Or is there a double agent in the marketing department at O?

Advertese isn't the language we speak at home. Advertese is the public language. Not that we speak it in public either. We

"Kissing Gouran..."

don't speak it, it screeches at us. It is the medium and therefore it is the message. And that's not news to anyone. It is FOX television; it is those jangly advertisements that frame Internet pages. Commercials have worked as mercilessly as Rohypnol, the date rape drug. Ads are anaesthetizing us, yet we claim we are deadening ourselves voluntarily to avoid their effects. If ads are everywhere, wouldn't we be numb all the time, voluntarily or involuntarily? If we can deliberately deaden ourselves to those swarming ads on the periphery of websites, when we walk down the street do we numb off and on like a strobe light? Or do we stay stupefied because our culture is still in a state of apocalypsis, where stupefied is normal?

If you grow up in Java, *Helostoma temminkii* are Natural. They have always flourished in shallow, sluggish, vegetated backwaters. In North American aquarium emporiums, they are called Balloon Body Pink Kissing Gouramis. You'll never get a school of them swimming in from the backyard next time your basement floods. If 500 years from now anyone happens to care, they might have to initiate a shopping cart pantheon Reformation, demanding that just because something is a product doesn't make it a divinity, that in fact hockey players, Elvis Impersonators, and Balloon Body Pink Kissing Gouramis do not belong in the product pantheon: they are living and respond to us. "Merchandise does not equal God," these reformers would say. That shopping cart pantheism can degenerate to the point of such a schism would pain my soul if I had one. Ads grow naturally in our streets, in our homes, and on our clothing. They were spawned in the think tanks of Madison Avenue, and now, as merchandisers say, they've got legs. By now every person born since 1984 assumes advertising is a natural feature of our North American environment. Consumer good gods can't possibly disturb our spiritual ecology.

And then there's the Subconscious: perhaps somewhere in the sluggish backwaters of our psyche we actually believe we deserve commercials. Commercials could be the penalty for materialism. Every time the commercial bullying begins, there might actually be a christianism in the Subconscious: "martyr," a vague remembrance of a sweet young man, eyes rolled back in his head, his whole torso stuck clear through with dozens of arrows. The words of Dietrich Bonhoeffer counsel us how to endure the punishment of advertising:

> One who lives … by grace is willing and ready to accept even insults and injuries without protest, taking them from God's punishing and gracious hand.[26]

PHOTOGRAPH ELEVEN:
Wee Beasties

Hanky in pocket I left room 7 again. For a while I stood on the corner of Tropicana Avenue. The vehicles lurched from red light to red light. When the light turned red at the intersection, I would look for amusing bumper stickers. It was not the bumper sticker set. I watched a hefty blue truck roll to a stop. The Great Seal of The State of Nevada was barely discernible on the side of the truck bed. The Great Seal must have been clawed by a grizzly bear. The picture on the dusty strips of peeling paper was homage to the nineteenth century mining industry and to a Roman aqueduct through majestic mountains. To a twenty-first century fifth grader, the farm implements in the foreground would probably be as mysterious as Heron's aeolipile of the first century CE. The perspective is just enough askew that these implements could be weapons, barbecue equipment, or fascinators. These old-fangled devices will incite poetry for generations to come. A notice was stuck next to The Great Seal: "Solid waste shall be loaded into box height not to exceed lid level." The truck bed was sturdy and deep. From where I stood, certainly there was no solid waste visible above lid level. Behind this workhorse-powered giant, there was a navy blue Audi A8, a silver BMW 7, a dark green Jaguar XJ, a black Mercedes-Benz S-Class, a white Lincoln Town Car, and a taupe Cadillac DTS. The dump truck carried Christian connotations. It was like a saviour carting away the sins of the flesh. Lined up behind this six-ton messiah, were the commuters clean and unburdened? I tried to imagine each car's solitary driver thinking, "How many times I have felt solid waste far exceed the lid level of my soul. Henceforth I shall live my life according to this vision of deliverance. I will place my faith in this: whatever is unclean can surely be hauled away."

Explanations of sin have always been contradictory. We inherited Adam's original sin. Supposedly, the Christ's sacrificial blood washed it away. But unless we believe this, the blood bath may not be ours to enjoy after all. Therefore the dirty piles of sin might keep building up till finally you die. Even if you are a believer, will dirty deeds not count as sins any more? Or is the washing process automatic every time you soil your soul? To me this wash-rinse-spin reasoning has always felt like motion sickness instead of what *mysterium stupendum* is supposed to feel like. *Mysterium stupendum* is spiritual astonishment. In the presence of something holy, the amazement is indescribable. When we encounter the "wholly other," words just won't do because the experience is beyond familiar, beyond intelligible, beyond natural.

Suppose a soul does get overloaded with guilt. The psyche is starting to tilt precariously. Once again psychoanalysts would be happy to review the psyche's situation. If the imbalance gets too nauseating to withstand, whether it's from sin or something else, the dread of mental capsize worsens. The anticipation of capsize gets too intense. At some point this dread has simply got to go. It must be forcefully ejected. Look! There's something out there onto which dread can be projected! The something could be cow meat, toy guns, communism, white sugar, pubic nudity, germs, anything really, but especially germs. Germs carry tons of dread on their tiny shoulderless bodies.

"A Bacterium or two"

The pagan ancients of Greece had supposedly projected their dread onto the *Keres*, "malignant little demons who brought illness, death and other troubles on mankind."[27] The Greeks endorsed fighting invisibility with invisibility. When invaded by *Keres*, the Greeks would call out to Herakles, an invisible Hero with "bluff good humour, readiness to help a friend and common sense."[28] Herakles, the Averter of Evil, would gladly eradicate the *Keres*. Herakles was the classic supernatural Mr. Clean. Back in the 1600s, van Leeuwenhoek had observed the *Keres* with his magnifying lens and called them "wee beasties." In retrospect this epithet is not as poetic as it seemed at the time. It was not until the turn of the nineteenth century that we humans finally got scientific proof that the *Keres* were real. Bacteria are wee beasts. In 1900 there remained no doubt: the germ theory was valid. That did it. "Unclean" shame was absolutely fused to uncanny "invisible."

Outside the hothouse of Christian theology, the idea of the invisible had gone feral; it had mutated. From the early twentieth century to today, whatever is invisible has become increasingly *unheimlich*. The invisible is not holy, it's disconcerting. Weird bacteria, with their abnormal sexuality, are sliming everywhere inside and outside homes, hospitals, and churches. Now the dread that the psychoanalysts blamed on guilt starts to feel quite rational. There's a problem to solve. Besides, even the first pope of the world wasn't great at self-psychoanalysis:

> Jesus called the crowd to him and said, "Listen and understand. What goes into a man's mouth does not make him 'unclean,' but what comes out of his mouth, that is what makes him 'unclean.'"
>
> ... Peter said, "Explain the parable to us."
>
> "Are you still so dull?" Jesus asked him. "Don't you see that whatever enters the mouth goes into the stomach and then out of the body? But the things that come out of the mouth come from the heart, and these make a man 'unclean.'"[29]

Without agreeing with me that product pantheism suits our contemporary nervous system, many have instinctively taken the advice from Pindar's pagan ode, "It is always best to look at whatever lies before our feet"[30]: the kitchen floor, the toilet bowl, the bottom of the tub. The fact that germs account for dread is a relief—and not a relief. Thankfully, invisible unicellular entities are not transcendent, yet they are truly a menace. They must be exorcized with mass-produced chemicals. The sickening little demons can be sprayed, mopped, dusted, wiped, swept, swiffered, and misted into oblivion. As for the unclean that is coming out of my mouth, coming from my unclean pantheistic heart, there is no scientific evidence it is contagious.

PHOTOGRAPH TWELVE:
Pandemonium

On the second morning, exiting the alley, I turned left again. I was going to keep on strolling down the boulevard in the holy land of hype. At first I judged The Strip as just another midway. Even though its hotels are as fat as Mount Rushmore, isn't it just an XXXL-size county fair? The Strip, however, is not a just-an anything. As an idea, Las Vegas is both flimsier and more imposing than a whole lot of different places not in Nevada.

Very soon I reached a site of architectural bedlam. In the distance I could still see the Eiffel Tower. In the foreground bunched together on the left I saw New York-New York Hotel & Casino and its Coney Island roller coaster, Manhattan City Hall, Chrysler Building, and Statue of Liberty. Adjacent to these

I could see the six pointy red turrets of The Excalibur Palace. Directly behind the Palace was The Hollywood Hotel. I could see a fifty-foot Devil Woman attacking the roof of Diablos Casino. The MGM Grand bulged in front. All of this was vertically bisected by a glade of palm trees and bisected horizontally by a four-lane freeway overpass.

In 1962 the Missouri-born theologian Richard Niebuhr died just before he would have had to face the *TIME* magazine portrait of his old pal Barth. Unlike Barth, Niebuhr would not have described the fifty-foot Devil Woman as a chthonic idol. And he would not have bemoaned the architectural pandemonium surrounding the Diablos building. Niebuhr was not in denial. He perceived pantheism in modern America.

> For the most part contemporary pantheism finds and experiences mysterious sublimity in the works of men—in great music, in the breath taking spans of great bridges, in soaring towers.[31]

Like Niebuhr I am an excessively educated North American type, and have been trained to see majestic aristocratic productions as mysteriously sublime. No matter how timeless the idea of devil, no matter how monumental in size, The Strip's fifty-foot Devil Woman's bust and butt are not what Niebuhr meant by breath-taking spans. A crisis of values could result from the spectacle of this Devil Woman atop the roof of a twenty-storey building. Is she sublime or is she carnivalesque? Is she big trivial? Is she post-modern awesome?

Alas, be reminded that this Devil Woman is no more tarted up with supernaturally crimson lips and Elizabethan Taylored eyebrows than was the twenty-five-foot Athena in the cella of the Parthenon. The so-called classical Greeks slapped on garish paint as enthusiastically as the Nevada Chamber of Commerce. Marshall McLuhan would have deemed the Athena marble medium to be as hot as the Devil Woman. McLuhan tried to warn us: high temperature *mysterium stupendum* doesn't ignite *caritas*. McLuhan predicted that when visual hyperbole predominates, compassion is burnt off.

I hadn't realized that The Pyramid and The Sphinx were further north of Diablos. Even if I had known this, Diablos and the surrounding visual mayhem were too much already. I needed to turn back to the Travelodge and rest my eyes.

PHOTOGRAPH THIRTEEN:
Dow Jones Concussion

Outdoors once again I meandered in a righterly direction. I noticed the *Las Vegas Review-Journal* headline, "U.S. financial crisis spreads around the world," then saw the headline of the *Las Vegas Sun*, "Visitors determined to have a good time, don't want to hear financial news." President George W. Bush's analysis of $1.2 trillion vanishing from the United States stock market in twelve hours: "a big problem."

After a long walk I saw a most peculiar pole. It was as tall and thick as a column, but it wasn't supporting a portico. It appeared to be sheathed in Mylar. Numerous colossal cylindrical, tubular, and boxy plastic forms were glommed onto it willy-nilly. Traffic lights were stuck to its sides. Digital screens the size of tennis courts jutted out. A ribbon of LED information twinkled along the bottom. I recognized that the LED was displaying NYSE data. It recorded **DJIA** ↓ 8378.95, followed by a silhouette of a bear. Above, on a digital screen, enclosed in a cartouche of curlicues and exclamation marks, shone the phrase ALL YOUR FAVOURITE GAMES. Quickly, this changed to Lee Harvey Oswald's face. The caption was "Back for Another Magical Season." I never can remember the name of the actual magician whose face it must have been.

The bailouts of the savings and loan institutions, big banks, and the auto industry would finally occur many weeks later. But before that, maybe in a midnight moment, a public relations maestro heard the shade of Bernays proclaim, "Win with this!—'too big to fail.'" What monstrous numbers must have-nots (consumers) total before we are the ones too big to fail? I don't know. I do know that in the 1950s Barth, the Niebuhr brothers, Paul Tillich, and the other star theologians talked like God was too big to fail.

For eons idolatry has been anathema to Judeo-Christian worshippers. The dualistic rhetoric of good God against evil idol was inherent to Judeo-Christian cosmology. Theologians have hissed about idolatry as if it was worse than syphilis. Materialistic pursuits would surely qualify as idol worship. The mid-century modern theologians, however, were reproaching materialism as a wrongheaded detour, rather than idolatry. It wasn't as if the theologians themselves were living like Okies. As long as consumer products had seemed to offer unprecedented promise and power they might rival the major traditional Christian claim: Jesus was supposed to be the one with the biggest promises and power. Considering Jesus was also God, he was the one who decided what real power was. Thus belief in the divine assets of Christianity would be necessary for a good life. But not so, it turned out, in order to live the modern post-apocalyptic dream. The status accruing from a 1957 red and white Corvette, a Brooks Brothers suit, or a Sheaffer Snorkel fountain pen also denoted power. Mid-century theologians did not catch on that material plenitude brought a good enough experience of power into a lot of people's lives. Purchasing power was obviously a kick, even if all a person bought was a bright yellow nylon cord. Divine power was so inconspicuous.

Most modernist theologians fudged the doctrine, however, by reviling attitudes, not personal behaviour, and certainly not vices. Medical scientists, not theologians, took control of the vices: compulsions are not gluttony or greed; a substance abuser is not a dope fiend, and so forth. Middle-class, highfalutin expenditure was exhibitionism said Thorstein Veblen. Yet none of the mid-century theologians specifically took a swipe at "conspicuous consumption," which in 1899 had become a recognized behaviour. The theologians condemned materialism *per se*, thinking perhaps that theatrical materialism was an epiphenomenon.

There was, and there remains to this very moment, an entire industry of moralists who condemn consumerism. Even hypocrites condemned it:

> The Whites have carried to these (colonial) people the worst that they could carry: the plagues of the world: materialism, fanaticism.[32]

In his 1958 book *The Affluent Society*, the economist John Kenneth Galbraith (1908-2006) actually predicted that a consumer society would end badly.

> The more goods people procure, the more packages they discard and the more trash that must be carried away. The counterpart of increasing opulence will be deepening filth. The greater the wealth the thicker will be the dirt.[33]

Galbraith tried to articulate in what way consumerism *per se* was becoming an ideology,

> A society which sets for itself the goal of increasing its supply of goods will tend, inevitably, to identify all innovation with addition to, changes in, or increase in its stock of goods.[34]

"The present cultural state of America would give us a good opportunity for studying the damage to civilization which is thus to be feared," said Freud.[35]

Consumerism may not have been a dominant way of life; statistically, it may not have been conspicuous enough even in the 1950s. But still it must have felt natural, given that post-apocalyptic regression was at its most inflamed. Everyone must have assumed consumerism was too superficial to breed gods.

No one could have predicted that commodity pantheism is only possible after an absolute glut of consumer products becomes the norm. These are the conditions that have created an infinity of purchasing-power moments. Such circumstances finally reveal that we can no longer identify benevolent deities by their limitless power. Especially now that we know what a Hydrogen Bomb can do.

Commodity pantheism is so much more by being so much less than mere commodity fetishism. Commodity fetishism, sickening as it is to Marxists, became a favourite trope of advertisers and it flourishes to this day as a classic rhetorical device. Although it cannot be proven that the companies promoting product love behave as if their employees are human resources instead of humans, advertising presumes that it is normal to adore a product as much as a family member. For example, in September 2014 a Hyundai Elantra television ad shows a young man removing a family portrait from the mantel of his MACtac brick fireplace and exchanging it for a picture of his new, bright blue Hyundai.

Commodity pantheism has nothing to do with loving a product as if it was human while treating humans like products. Commodity fetishism may be happening every hour of every day, but I am saying commodity pantheism has nothing to do with love.

Commodity pantheism has been sitting pretty in the North American Subconscious like a chronic case of pork worm. After pork tapeworms wriggle up to the brain, they

"Tapeworm"

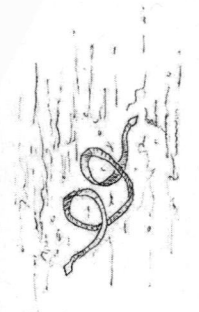

> ... do not want to be detected by the immune system, because then they will most likely be eaten by phagocytes and die. They try to do everything they can to avoid eliciting a strong immune response. Parasite larvae also don't want to do anything that can kill the host. If the host dies, then the parasites die too. For this reason, people can have parasites for years and not show any symptoms at all. But then, as the larval defenses break down, the host immune system is able to have a greater effect, and the symptoms become more obvious.[36]

Commodity pantheism, however, is not as primitive as a larva. Larval defence breakdown provoking the host immune reaction to intensify till symptoms become more obvious is a fine analogy, up to the point of autoimmune death. If I were a theologian, I would proclaim that there are invasions by parasites of all kinds, including oil companies, careless nuclear plant contractors, climate change deniers, and Ponzi schemers; if I were a psychoanalyst, I would claim commodity pantheism may prove itself a salvation to twenty-first century psyches. And the reason is that we are no longer humans, we are human resources. We are no longer customers, we are consumers. We are no longer go-getters, we must always be on the go; wearing blue jeans on the go, eating energy bars on the go, texting on the go, deodorizing ourselves because we are on the go, throwing pods into washing machines because powder or fluid is too complicated when you are on the go. These changes have poisoned relationships. This poison is wearing us down. Shopping cart pantheism is easy; it requires no energy. It won't wear you down. It goes with everything even when you are on the go, but also when you are not. It's about time something was actually free and actually easy. It's about time there's a form of holiness that isn't hype.

The mid-century theologians kept insisting that the most meaningful and powerful deity will eternally triumph. The most effective God with the most staying power is supposed to win; this had been the expected behaviour for a genuine deity in the thousands of eons before the Jesus cult cropped up. Effective staying power is definitely what you want in a car wax. Godly goods, accessible as they are, have an effect that advertisers always evade: these overabundant gods don't care about you. They are inanimate. They cannot care about you. You can love them but they won't love back. To Christian theologians this was supposed to be proof of their emptiness. But this is the most significant attribute of these gods: every manufactured object is a lesson in humility, a reminder that no matter how you feel toward them, it just isn't going to register. If they don't or can't care, what next? That's the beauty of it. What next? Nothing. What could be more relaxing?

There is, however, an actual lesson to be learned. Post-apocalyptic delusions of omnipotence and of omniscience will be met with a product's dead passivity. This is what can be humbling about products. The theologian Thomas Merton (1915-1968) put a lot of emphasis on humility, and rightly so in a post-apocalyptic age. "Humility makes us real," he said. It's not rare to get humiliated, but to be humbled, that's refreshing. The mid-century modernist theologians hadn't separated being humble from their intricate system of beliefs. It's just that the feeling of being humbled doesn't require belief any more. Being humbled is an emotional reaction. It is of course no justification for becoming a shopping cart pantheist. That's the attraction of shopping cart pantheism. It has no justification whatsoever. It's an option like everything else.

PHOTOGRAPH FOURTEEN:
Being and Thingness

Mid-century theologians were convinced that human beings cannot worship an inanimate object. In his Introduction to *Portrait of Karl Barth*, Robert McAfee Brown said that for Barth "the worst sin possible [is] that of transforming a man-made product into something divine."[37]

The august Martin Buber (1878-1965), speaking only for himself, said, "God can never become an object for me."[38] On top of that, Buber also condemned concept worship:

> The more abstract the concept, the more does it need to be balanced by the evidence of living experience with which it is intimately bound up rather than linked in an intellectual system.[39]

Strictly speaking, I had not purchased Buber's *The Eclipse of God* on impulse. I had been stumbling around in second-hand bookstores in a variety of cities for almost three years looking for anything published by Buber. I knew full well that *I and Thou* was the book a historian was supposed to want. The poet's attitude, however, is that a chance benefit is sweeter than a premeditated one. And if you are going to pervert someone's lifetime of thought, why be picky? Richard Niebuhr's brother Reinhold has a promotional blurb on the back cover of Buber's *The Eclipse of God*. Reinhold declared Buber "The greatest living Jewish Philosopher."

For a few weeks I did not read anything but that very phrase on the book's back cover. This was demanding. The cover design is a purple and black egg-and-dart motif that seems to be cloning itself every ten minutes. Risking macular degeneration, I stared at the phrase "The greatest living Jewish Philosopher." If I looked away, the phrase would have become abstract. I kept it in front of my face to secure its status as the evidence of living experience with which it is intimately bound. Hadn't this description been properly reviewed by a clear-headed editor?

The greatest. Could not Reinhold Niebuhr possibly have said, "in my opinion"? Could he just maybe have said, "I admire Buber as …"?

living. What was Niebuhr insinuating would happen when Buber died? Would Buber decompose among the thousands of ordinary Jewish philosophers? Is there only one dead Jewish philosopher who is the greatest? And therefore was Reinhold

Niebuhr implicitly telling Buber, "Marty, as long as you are living, fine, but for a dead Jewish philosopher Spinoza can't be beat."

Jewish. Was Reinhold Niebuhr, whether he intended to or not, likening Buber to this year's minor league MVP?

Buber wrote about the worldly smokescreens billowing against the face of God. In his earthy yet eloquent way, Buber could name the obfuscations available in the modern age. The eclipse of God was darkening the twentieth century soulscape, and Heideggerian philosophy wasn't making things brighter. In the midst of Buber's tenderly chosen words about polytheism, he quoted Heidegger, "The appearing of God and gods may dawn again."[40] Buber was a thorough and honest philosopher, so he acknowledged Heidegger on this point. And Buber felt not an iota of ambivalence: a multiplicity of gods is utterly fanciful, even if Heidegger had said it.

Heidegger's elucidation, or was it obfuscation, I don't have the faintest idea which, of *Being* was a theological jackpot. For Buber it was a noun, a synonym for God: "knowable Being, from whom all meaning comes." For others a God as "the ground of all Being," a concept familiar to the Greek philosophers, was rejuvenated because it alluded to Heidegger's *oeuvre*. It was a signal you had brains if you could allude to Heidegger. Buber, however, did not worry for one minute that inanimate objects are an aspect of Being, that objects have Being. That they exist was good enough Being. Buber called Heidegger's bluff: That Heidegger's *Being* "means anything other than the inherent fact of all existing being, namely, that it exists, remains insurmountably empty."[41]

"Mood Ring"

If existing is all that is required as Being, any old object has it: pliers, mood rings, flea collars. Any new object has Being too. Old or new they got their Being, every last one of them. At least on that account, mass-produced products cannot be disqualified as deities. Why wouldn't consumer goods qualify as "the realer religion … cease[ing] to be the special domain 'Religion' and will[ing] to become life?"[42]

Buber had a profound understanding of religion, too profound to exclude an idea that could be ridiculously misinterpreted. If "life" is realer religion beyond Religion's own nominal territory, what do we find but a domain cluttered with consumer goods? Anyway, a great many theologians have posited that sometimes exactly because a belief is ridiculous, fidelity to it is all the more valid. The first such opinion on record is from the second century CE; Tertullian's *Credo quia absurdum* proclaims, "I believe because it is absurd."[43] Paul Tillich's wishy-washy expression for this: "There is no faith without an intrinsic 'in spite of.'"[44] Pee-wee Herman said, "Everybody's got a big But."[45]

PHOTOGRAPH FIFTEEN:
Under the Monorail

Just before twilight I was standing at the causeway of the Khnum sphinxes. It was a curved sidewalk turning blue in the suffocating heat. The seven dwarf sphinxes lining the causeway were in the form of sheep-headed kittens. A stiff stone pharaoh doll was trapped under each sphinx chin. The causeway sidewalk swerved abruptly left just where the row of sphinxes abutted a trash bin. A concrete, undersized Ramses II was enthroned to the left of the trash bin. His sightline traversed the seven sphinx buttocks to focus on a Hooters bar across the boulevard. Fruit sprigs of a dozen palm trees began to glow gold in a nearby grove of streetlights. Gingerly, I lifted my eyes. The pyramid filled the sky. The glassy pyramid was midnight purple. It was a behemoth of geometry. A solarized-pink body of a half-naked man was projected on its surface. The pyramid was staging a translucent 350-foot ad for a magic show. (A few months later I found the magician's website. The website background music is the sound of a hundred girls squealing. One of his specialties as a conjuror includes "6 Ways to Cheat Death.")

Stage right The Las Vegas Sphinx rises two times taller than its sand-swept ancestor at Giza. Unlike the original the nose and ornamental beard are still on the head. The expression is absentminded. The flat blue eyes are in the grip of some very severe eyeliner. Otherwise the monster is a pumpkin colour. Piercing this hypnagogic scene was the Mandalay Bay elevated monorail.

I walked over and paused under the monorail. I could hear it whirring. In moments the Mandalay Bay train swished overhead. In moments it was elsewhere. Freud's metaphor of the Subconscious as ancient city was left shuddering in contrails. Paul Tillich's rhetoric, which in my opinion displays major symptoms of post-apocalyptic regression, emphasized:

> The disrupting trends of man's consciousness are one of the great problems of all personal life. If a uniting center is absent, the infinite variety of the encountered world, as well as the inner movements of the human mind, are able to produce or complete the disintegration of the personality.[46]

In Las Vegas it is demonstrated that a disintegrated psyche has become normal.

Suppose that in our twenty-first century psyches the monorail, a twentieth century object, has no history. It is not, in other words, an object about which we reminisce. It is not an image that connects with any remarkable moment leading up to Y2K. Maybe the monorail will someday gain a history, but likely that will come one individual psyche at a time. The Egyptian pyramids, in contrast, already have a shared history, at least as an image. When you are actually standing there, Las Vegas's very own humongous midnight-purple pyramid will definitely become one heck of an experience. This just might be its only history for that person. It may be an idiosyncratic, individualistic experience. It may be "just like on the website!" But it will be an experience. The Mandalay Bay monorail will hang right there in front of it.

Freud's depiction of the Subconscious was elegant. Twenty-first century consciousness could be described elegantly if a poet ever wanted to. Elegantly or not the twenty-first century consciousness easily hosts a myriad of incongruent objects and moments. Children may not like their food touching, but they enter the twenty-first century soon enough. Here, experiences can all intermix anachronistically in the same brain bowl.

After time spent contemplating the pyramid and sphinx, I decided to cross The Strip. I found a stairway to the pedestrian overpass. At the pinnacle of the stairway, a digital billboard glittered with recurring images. A repeating video clip from a sexy floor show was inserted between ads for sunscreen, wedding photography, hamburgers, helicopter rides, diamond rings, and drugstores. The floorshow ad previewed frenzied dancing triplets in black ultra-petite tube tops and white-fringed bikini bottoms. The dancers' hairdos were as if they were wearing

"Martini Glass"

bright red blowfish on their heads. The triplets' outfits were alike in every visible detail as they pranced in a line, yet their posture and gestures were haphazard. They were brandishing electric guitars. Unlike drum majorettes who synchronize their batons, the chorus girls were swirling their guitars indiscriminately. The background was a whirlpool of contracting and dilating circles, the colours pulsating from orange with blue to black with pink and back again.

This showtime sampler would reappear predictably between the hamburger and the helicopter rides. The effect of the repetition was as if there was an endless supply of dancers. They were exemplary as the standardized angels of mass production. They were Madonnas of the assembly line. These frolicking emissaries of late capitalism were as persistent as the ticking of a clock. They were inexorable; they conjured a new form of eternity.

I glanced at my wristwatch. Time may be a so-called timeless concept; that does not mean I understand how this concept refers to anything but pragmatism. I do perceive change, but the concept of Time is uncanny. Whether it is the hands or the electronic numbers, something is regularly and eternally changing on a clock face. These are among the universal illustrations of the concept of time. It is extremely difficult to ignore these so-called chronological movements when everyone else on the planet believes in them. I'm not saying I want to ignore mass hysteria. There's nothing intrinsically shameful about mass hysteria. If it's helpful to others I pay attention to the clock.

Time is honoured so seriously that it must surely be an example of what Buber eschewed: concept worship. It's not because I am spiritually comparable to Buber that I avoid concept worship; it's because concepts are invisible. I certainly know that I would not qualify as a practising polytheist in Niebuhr's terms. Time is one of the masterworks of human consciousness; as a man-made phenomenon it has a breathtaking span. But, like an insect, though for different reasons, Time doesn't belong in the consumer product pantheon. Yes, it's a human invention. No, it's not alive. It has no psyche. It doesn't answer us and it doesn't answer to us. You cannot destroy it. It is humbling. It's magnificent. But it's disembodied. It's not made out of anything. You can't stare at it. When I think of it I am filled with awe. The concept of Time is overwhelming. And that's my problem, the infirmity of my anemic soul. I haven't got the spirit to tackle transcendence.

My wristwatch is altogether another matter; my wristwatch is one of my shopping cart deities. It is a 1974 men's windup Timex with a bistre brown leather band. When I bought this lifeless mass-marketed item at the Salvation Army second hand store in Ithaca, New York, in 1979 perhaps you would have predicted that eventually I would find a new timepiece more stylish, or more convenient, more contemporary. You may have predicted that if a portable telephone that could keep time was invented, I would buy one like everybody else was going to. I wouldn't expect you to have known back in 1979 that I was unselfconsciously, inherently a shopping cart pantheist. I soon stopped winding the Timex. A product deity is not valuable because of its usefulness to humans. Uselessness, I can guarantee, is unprecedented in the history of the popular gods. The selling point of a new god has always been its superiority over other modes of usefulness, including over any magic in the neighbourhood. Such as when Barnabas and St. Paul

> traveled through the whole island of Cyprus until they came to Paphos. There they met a Jewish sorcerer and false prophet named Bar-Jesus, who was an attendant of the proconsul Serius Paulus. The proconsul, an intelligent man, sent for Barnabas and Paul because he wanted to hear the word of God. But the sorcerer opposed them and tried to turn the proconsul from the faith. Then Paul, filled with the Holy Spirit, looked straight at the sorcerer and said "You are a child of the devil and an enemy of everything.... You are going to be blind, and for a time you will be unable to see the light of the sun." Immediately mist and darkness came over him and he groped about seeking someone to lead him by the hand. When the proconsul saw what happened, he believed, for he was amazed.[47]

Shopping cart pantheism is not based on admiration of power. These consumer gods don't have to prove useful. They don't have anything to prove. When I want to use a commodity, my Coolpix for instance, no blasphemy is implied; actually using the camera is just less apathetic. When I utilize one of the product deities, it's not an impure act; it's more like a spiritual complication. There's nothing intrinsically sacrilegious about complications—in anything really, not for a poet.

When I glance at my Timex I see the face of a god. It doesn't look back at me. If it did it wouldn't be a god. When it doesn't see me I feel humbled. Here is the impassive god who cannot care what you do. Divinity comes in so many shapes and sizes. Buy them. Don't buy them. Buying one of them doesn't have anything to do with pantheism. It's their numbers that save you the effort of making a pilgrimage, or making any move whatsoever. And don't be fooled that shopping cart pantheism is therefore a time saver. Time can't be saved. Merchandise can be saved.

PHOTOGRAPH SIXTEEN:
The Crow and the Fish

I had crossed the boulevard and turned back southward. I walked through sundown. Already the rush hour traffic was loud. The evening was getting gritty and stayed very hot. I was walking and thinking. The interior of my mind was airtight at body temperature. My thoughts were dust-free and formless. As I was passing a construction site, I sensed something scuffling in the gravel behind a wire fence. It was a crow. The crow was jabbing its beak into half a bagel. The crow steadied the bagel with one foot. The foot was swollen, pale, and scaly. It didn't look painful. It looked strangely adaptive. It looked like an itty-bitty *Tyrannosaurus rex* claw. The bird was concentrating on the bagel as anyone would in a matter of life and death. Or professionalism. Or pride. Or stubbornness. Or maternal love.

Or curiosity. Or centre of ultimate concern. "Ultimate concern," one of the unsmiling standards of Paul Tillich's theological oratory, "includes total surrender to the content of this concern."[48] The crow appeared to surrender totally to the content of the bagel. The bagel seemed to be the crow's ultimate concern, well, for the moment.

A crow is a consumer just like the rest of us. Still, we cannot claim we know 100 per cent that the crow experiences a bagel only in terms of nutrition and energy. At the moment of pure focus, the bagel's content could imply, according to Tillich, faith. Tillich expressly stated, "There is no faith without a content toward which it is directed."[49] I didn't presume, as Freud would have, that crow Id-oil pressure equilibrated with the Reality Principle at the exact moment crow-Ego was dominating the object-bagel. Though I do know the crow did not benefit from my intelligence or good will.

So the bagel was a demonstration of the mechanics of faith according to Tillich. As for the crow, it was not a snow-white dove. For an instant, for symbolic consistency, I had wished that the bird had at least been a pigeon, a rock dove technically. But of what use are technicalities for poets? Technicalities become prosaic quicker than Dr. Bruce Banner can swell up and turn green.

Next I noticed a wide five-foot long plastic pipe at the south end of the site. Its original silvery surface probably had been shiny. Now it lay in a mauve and yellow cloud of exhaust fumes and sand. On it, to my surprise, I perceived an impression of a large fish, just faint enough that I wasn't sure whether it had been stencilled or was somehow drawn in powder. It was incomplete, as eroded fossils tend to be. Actually, I looked closer to confirm the image could not possibly be a fossil, the pipe not in fact an oblong rock. The eye of the fish was prominent as if at the moment of death it had gawped in disbelief. All the scales along the backbone and at the base of the tail were distinct. They were almost like droplets, suggesting a rainy-day surface-feeding fish. The faint shape of the tail was oddly marked by crisscrosses. No fins were visible. My first reaction was to equate this image with the iconic fish I'd seen scratched into stone at St. Domitilla's catacomb in Rome. Given the time and distance between Rome and Las Vegas, the striking resemblance was rather unnerving, until I reminded myself that edible fish seldom differ when served on a plate. St. Domitilla's fish had also lacked fins. Otherwise, the Las Vegas fish looked like it might have been a particular species, a lanky fish with a strong wide tail. St. Domitilla's fish was more strictly symbolic. Its scales were unnaturally large and there were fewer of them. There was a minimum of detail, much like the outline of fish in colouring books. As a picture, the Las Vegas fish must have been derived from a machine-cut stencil because there were no irregularities. The identical scales were precisely the same distance apart. Of course St. Domitilla's fish would had been chiselled with an unwieldy dull edge.

I stood awhile in a contemplative state. A reverie began with the idea that like "Kilroy was here" in the 1950s, fish in 150

CE also marked someone's presence. I know that in the earliest times of the Jesus cult, an anchor might also be graven alongside the fish. Lambs, doves, the ☧, and eventually crosses would signal places of Christian congregation. I contrasted these ancient simple sigils with informative Depression-era hobo drawings on walls, sidewalks, and billboards. In some situations a drawing of a cross could mean, "Talk religion get food." Three little slash marks inside an oval meant a loaf of bread might be available. There was a diagram that translated "bad water." Understandably, there were hundreds of hobo signs, and for obvious reasons they would vary.

The prejudice against outlaw Early Christians differed from attitudes toward Depression-era hobos. At first the earliest Christians were inconspicuous. Unlike Serapean or Dionysian meetings, the Jesus gatherings quietly proceeded without dancing, serpents, or billowing smoke. It was what Christians did not do that was quite obvious and obviously scandalous: they skipped the emperor worship; if there was a festival for one of the Olympian gods Christians stayed home. Their absence from these public festivities was judged to be atheism. The Christians' refusal to serve in the military was treasonous. The usual cheap rumours of indecency circulated, that these mysterious fanatics fed upon their enemies and enjoyed sex with their siblings.

The plight of the hobos was not mysterious. In effect hobos *were* the symbols; they were icons of vulnerability and homelessness. A hobo could just as well have been the neighbour's oldest son who drifted out of town and returned one year later more ragged and just as jobless as ever.

As a shopping cart pantheist, I am as inconspicuous as the earliest Christians. In contrast to Christians, and to hobos as well, if there is another shopping cart pantheist in the vicinity we are in no hurry to get together. The most suspicious activity in which I indulge as a product pantheist is my wandering around in swanky stores without ever bringing an item to the cash register; I look like an indecisive shoplifter. Only I don't want to actually take anything. To take possession of any of these things is no fun; it's too tiring to think about. Visual appreciation is more than enough energy expenditure. Many North Americans feel normal and happy with their shopping cart filled. Again, that's not the point. The point is they don't know their shopping cart is chock full of gods.

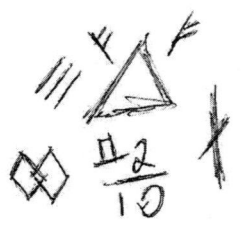

"series of Hobo symbols"

President George W. Bush's advice a few days after September 11, 2001, will never be forgotten, although I have forgotten his precise words. He counselled all Americans to go into the shopping malls like on any other ordinary day, and to continue to do so, presumably, in the decades to come. Fortunately, not having planned to shop or absolutely refusing to do so was not denounced as collaboration with the Taliban. Bush's reflex advice may have foreshadowed the evolution of consumerism into the State Religion. Galbraith had foreseen how abstention from conspicuous consumption would incur the label "indecent."

> People are poverty-stricken when their income, even if adequate for survival, falls markedly behind that of the community. Then they cannot have what the larger community regards as the minimum necessary for decency; and they cannot wholly escape therefore, the judgment of the larger community that they are indecent.[50]

It would be perverse if consumerism becomes North America's official religion and shopping cart pantheism its official creed. At first citizens jabbering cheerfully about the plenitude of mass-produced gods might seem celebratory. But if someone obviously never bothers to buy any of them, will that citizen be condemned as a hypocrite? How many generations before such a shopping cart teetotaller is branded, so to speak, as an atheist?

At present, like birdwatching, trying to spot a product pantheist requires knowledge of their identifying marks and behaviours. For instance, the clothes of a product pantheist might attract attention, but have nothing to do with a love of shopping; as for me, the archetypical product pantheist, I never show up in new clothes. Acquaintances probably assume it's a neurosis. I guarantee that product pantheism is the opposite of a neurosis. It is in fact a cure for post-apocalyptic regression. An obvious clue that you are in the presence of a product pantheist would be to hear lavishly detailed appreciation of a pretty little object such as a key chain made in Japan; yet it is soon revealed the rhapsodist did not buy the thing. Upon learning this you might feel a disillusioning pang of pointlessness. That pang will be your clue you are in the presence of a shopping cart pantheist.

Even if there is something austere or idiosyncratic about a product pantheist's interior decorating, you cannot conclude it adds up to product pantheism when it could just as easily be minimalism. Minimalism itself is a red herring. Minimalism has nothing to do with shopping cart pantheism, yet a shopping cart pantheist could coincidentally be a minimalist. If a genuine product pantheist's home does display a cornucopia of objects, there's no way of distinguishing this from plain old post-apocalyptic consumerism. The habitat of the shopping cart pantheist is just not going to reveal how much worship is going on. Visual clues are nonexistent; social clues are nonexistent: there is no symbolic jewellery; there are no meeting places and thus no typical architecture; and there are no classic scriptural phrases. Well, actually, everyone everywhere occasionally talks the lingo of shopping cart pantheism:

... when there is no tomorrow
... let your fingers do the walking
... reach out and touch someone
... just do it
... finger lickin' good

Slogans and jingles are scripture that hasn't been collated and never will be.

A jingle started to emerge from a crevice in my amygdala: "I wish I was an Oscar Mayer wiener." I blinked, shook my head, and listened intently to the noise of the traffic. Alert once again to my surroundings, I re-examined the dust fossil. There was a tiny rectangle I hadn't originally noticed near the tail. Inside the rectangle I was able to perceive *Skechers*. The fish icon was a print in the dust from the bottom of a running shoe.

I scurried forward and soon could see the Statue of Liberty. I decided to stop briefly to take a quick photograph or two. The Las Vegas statue is a half-size fibreglass and Styrofoam replica of the 1886 copper-clad original in New York. From across The Strip, I took a picture of her as she waved her torch from behind a palm tree. In proportion to the forty-five-storey hotel behind her, this Miss Liberty is a dainty marzipan bride stuck into a frosting of cement. Closer to her the Coney Island roller coaster twists and coils like a python eager to loop around its prey. At the statue's elbow, eight dazzling spotlights on a pole angle away from her face to exacerbate the glare of a manganese green **!!!24-HR BUFFET!!!** sign.

PHOTOGRAPH SEVENTEEN:
Miss Liberty

In *The New Testament*, John 14, Philip said,

"Lord, show us the Father and that will be enough for us."

Jesus answered: "Don't you know me, Philip, even after I have been among you such a long time? Anyone who has seen me has seen the Father. How can you say 'Show us the Father'?"

The same thing happened to the United States Postal Service. In 2010 they requested that Getty Images send them a stock photograph of the Statue of Liberty. Since 1847 the Postal Service had issued twenty-three Statue of Liberty stamps. This adds up to one new Statue of Liberty stamp every seven years. Seven was considered by the Pythagoreans to be a virgin number because it cannot be multiplied to produce any number within ten. The wife numbers are the numbers that can multiply to produce a number within ten: two (two copulates with two to produce four), three (three also copulates with two to produce six; three copulating, so to speak, with itself begets nine), and four (four copulating with two begets eight). In our era two times two and three times three would be considered cloning, not starting a family. These would become significant facts to any Pythagoreans in the United States Postal Service design department, especially when the boss says, "Hey, let's do another Statue of Liberty. It's been about seven years, hasn't it?" In December 2010 the twenty-fourth Statue of Liberty stamp was minted. It is one of those "forever" stamps. Twenty-four cannot be divided by seven and come out even.

Instead of a picture of the Progenitor (in New York), Getty Images sent the Las Vegas version (technically the daughter, not the only begotten son). The Postal Service was put in the position of quoting John 14 or the vernacular equivalent, "You seen one, you seen 'em all."

Reuters reported the situation to the world:

> New USA First Class stamps bearing an image of the Statue of Liberty were issued in December 2010, showing a low-angled close-up of Lady Liberty's face and crown. The image shown on the stamp is actually a photo of the replica standing outside the New York-New York Hotel & Casino in Las Vegas.
>
> The United States Postal Service became aware of what it is calling a "mischaracterization" in May 2011.... News of the

mix-up was first reported in the latest issue of Linn's Stamp News, a magazine for stamp enthusiasts.

The differences are subtle: the eyebrows and eyes of the replica are a little more sharply defined and she has a small rectangular patch that the original lacks on the central spike of the crown. The younger Las Vegas model also looks more fresh-faced, whereas the 124-year-old New Yorker is showing her age with darker-colored streaks on her nose and cheeks.

"French Fries"

The Reuters news item contains nine facts. I haven't yet decided in what way this is related to the virginity of the number seven. Each of these facts—any fact, really—is like a hot greasy French fry. Each fry would of course be different from the next, but it doesn't take a master's degree in engineering to analyze the difference. Facts are as simple to consume as a French fry. Everybody loves a fact and you can consume many more of them than French fries before you need an antacid. This is a good-enough simile for mass-marketed images too. Unlike French fries mass-marketed images ever so briefly evoke ideas. We wouldn't expect them to document something. Documentation is the honourable and hopeless task of historiographers. Evoking ideas is the task of poets. Maybe a poet has that job in the Statue of Liberty department at Getty Images. All poets know how to create an idea that appears to be a fact. A poetic illusion that appears to be a fact is no less welcome, and poets hope that a poetic illusion is just as stirring. Mistakes are very entertaining poetic illusions. The Miss Liberty stamp of December 2010 is fun for absolutely everybody because now we know the stamp must simply carry on "forever" being what it factually isn't.

The "mischaracterization" of Miss Liberty Las Vegas on the first-class forever stamp enacts exactly what Las Vegas itself is all about. Las Vegas designers and engineers make a 110 per cent effort to erect stupendous copies. Miss Liberty Las Vegas, and now her very own stamp portrait, is like Holly Golightly in *Breakfast at Tiffany's*. Yeah, she's a phony, but she's a *real* phony. As I have said, or implied, everything built is that kind of phony.

The United States Postal Service has embraced this brilliant mistake. The last word from them: "We love the stamp!" As if loving it undoes the ineptitude. In the old days they would have at least expressed chagrin. Prior to the Crash of 2008, their budget could have been huge enough to afford recalling all three billion of the stamps and starting over. Then, whatever number of mischaracterization stamps got into circulation would have stimulated the philatelic market. But these are the new days. The boss of the United States Postal Service is at the behest of a christianism; the delusion of omnipotence frees him or her to transform the reality of carelessness into the pleasure of commodity fetishism. The Postal Service loves the stamp. Of course they do. All of North America will love this stamp. It's because of the christianisms stuck to our souls. The stamp embodies the entire history of Christian art: copies of Jesus based on copies of Jesus based on copies of Jesus, and copies of Mother Mary based on copies of Mother Mary, and copies of Matthew, Mark, Luke, and John, and on and on and The Holy Spirit, based on—and on and on … forever. The stamp is also an exemplar of a vague jot of New Testament advice. If you want to see a god look at the most compelling replica you can get. As Jesus said to Philip in John 14...

PHOTOGRAPH EIGHTEEN:
It's All Good

First thing in the morning I crossed over Las Vegas Boulevard on one of the east-west pedestrian overpasses and then walked south. As I lingered on a south by southeast corner I could see a clarion scarlet sign between two white pilasters with gleaming gold Corinthian capitals. Without the possessive apostrophe the words stood confidently vibrant. CAESARS PALACE. CAESARS without the apostrophe is all-inclusive, like MEN or CABALLEROS on restroom doors. Just as I read the word *CAESARS* I clearly saw that the next word to its right was *RUMP*. Obviously I was standing at just the necessary angle for the wall of Caesars Palace to block the left end of the Trump Tower's rooftop sign. I then experimented with crouching while otherwise not changing position. From this lower angle, one of the CAESARS lofty flame cauldrons would also obscure the first two letters of a glittering casino name on a building between the other two. Because on this third building's sign the two letters *MI* were hidden, the three different signs aligned horizontally to present the silly idea of "Caesars rump rage." I was startled, and not because of the puerile phrase I had assembled; I was surprised that I hadn't intuitively projected or composed a phrase with Christian connotations.

There is no question that the fragment was psychoanalytically significant. In his own terms, Freud had analyzed the profound implications of rump rage. Rump rage is a poetic expression for "the anal phase," the developmental period when an infant has enough coordination to walk, to mimic its parents' actions, and learn to use a toilet. Freud was certain that the latter aspect of infant development was noteworthy. It is a phase when the toddler's bowel control can get ferocious. In today's conversation the phrase "anal-retentive" is a mild or vindictive insult depending on tone of voice. This epithet derives from Freud's observation that some toddlers will use their poo as self-expression. Some express anger by leaving their poo strewn about ("anal expulsive") and some show defiance with voluntary constipation. It is intriguing that "anal-expulsive" is not heard on the street nearly as often as "anal-retentive." Suddenly self-conscious, I stood up from my squatting position.

Even if it wasn't immediately evident to me, I was not ready to admit there was no Christian connection to my musings. I was determined to stand there pondering the scene indefinitely until relevance to Jesus emerged. Sensational memories, however, soon dissipated my plan. Reminiscence of Rome captivated my attention. The grandeur that was Rome dominated my mindscape. Whether or not I actually closed my eyes, I no longer saw Las Vegas. I was remembering how I had meandered through Trastevere late one afternoon. I had been looking for Via della VII Coorte, the address of the Excubitorium so famous for its ancient graffiti. Complaints and vulgarities were apparently scratched on the barrack walls by third century firefighters stationed there. Before I had located Via della VII Coorte, I got distracted by a tutti-frutti gelato in a cappuccino bar. And then I got lost. The only Excubitorium graffiti I would ever know would be the sentence I had read on the Internet, which was *omnia tuta*. It literally means "It's all safe," but it could be slang. It could be ironic, like the way Bob Dylan sings, "It's all good."

Irony led me just where it always does, down into my Subconscious. Immediately, I recalled a glossy photograph between pages 64 and 65 in my copy of *Greek Thought and the Rise of Christianity*.[51] The photograph documents a chunk of graffiti uncovered in Rome in 1857. A sketch had been gouged into the northwest wall of room 7 in The Palace of the Caesars. The image had been incised on the surface with a finely sharpened implement. It is an engraved cartoon of a crucifixion. The victim is shown from the rear. The drawing of his rump is blatant. He has the head of a donkey. I don't know where I read it, so it may not be a fact, but victims of crucifixion supposedly weren't issued a loincloth. If this is so, the graffiti was full rear view nudity. Would drawing a butt instead of genitals imply a bashful graffitist? Quite the curiosity: a prim vandal.

Church historians insist this cartoon is mocking first century Jesus worship. In any commentary I have read, the Egyptian god Set isn't considered as an alternative object of scorn. Set is traditionally described as having a donkey head on a human body. Official Egyptian depictions of Set were very precisely detailed, but not scientific. Set's official inhuman head resembles an aardvark as closely as it resembles a donkey. In other words, there's some poetry to Set's persona. Or maybe it's comparable to the ancient Hebrews always saying *Adonai* because God's true name is too sacred to speak aloud. Set was the god of chaos, storms, and darkness. Maybe the Egyptians assumed they would be safer with a deliberate mischaracterization of Set. He was so mean; if he didn't like his picture taken by humans, his rage could be awful. It does seem the Egyptian gods were not omniscient. It is not clear they could read. So actually, Set might be the last one to know the official hieroglyphs were all about him.

The victim on the cross in the satirical cartoon is conspicuously donkey-headed, so this must be what the church scholars interpret as ridicule. Also, they are historians. They scrutinize the provenance, the papyri, and the archaeological fragments.

There's a caption scrawled under the cartoon. Presumably, it refers to the curly-haired guy who's waving to Mr. Donkey-Head: "ΑΛΕΞΑΜΕΝΟΣ ΣΕΒΕΤΕ ΘΕΟΝ." This can be translated as "Alexamenos respect god." Actually, the historians translate it as "Alexamenos worships his god." This probably demonstrates their expertise with ancient Greek. Or it could be they're compensating for the graffitist's having skipped grammar class.

PHOTOGRAPH NINETEEN:
Second Century CET
(Current Era of the Transistor)

Between 474 and 462 BCE, Pindar wrote odes celebrating victories in the Olympian, Nemean, and Pythian games. It was not hubris that spurred the contestants in boys' boxing, mule-cart racing, armoured running, and so forth. Victory by strength, grace, and courage was a tribute to The Immortals, not in any way a challenge to them:

> Seek not to become Zeus!
> You have everything if but a share
> Of these beautiful things comes to you.[52]

For many centuries the psychological connotations of the word "ambition" were the same as for "hubris." Priests of the fifteenth century were still denouncing ambition as "pride and vainglory." Maybe it was not until the eighteenth century that the word "ambition" lost its moral roughage. "Ambition," from the mouths of colonial warlords and pirates, began to mean what it means today, and to consumers of status especially.

Neither ambition nor hubris is the same as an omnipotence fantasy. A psychoanalyst could claim that the superheroes in mass or myth media are the best evidence for omnipotence fantasies, originating of course in the Subconscious Id. Poets always depicted Herakles, Theseus, and Orestes as invincible. The unique powers of Superman, the X-Men, The Incredible Hulk, *et al.* surpass by far the human muscularity of athletes such as Muhammad Ali, Marshawn Lynch, or Sydney Crosby. Consider, for instance, "I could ice him no problem." A psychoanalyst might say this shameful Id omnipotence fantasy can be projected from the psyche, thrown out forcibly, and reappear in the image of superhuman fictional characters. I get it as an explanation for a Greek psyche up to 500 BCE, when hubris was dangerous and shameful. But that's assuming Greek citizens even had a Subconscious. In the twentieth century—and nowadays—is it really necessary to deny omnipotence fantasies? Is lust for power unseemly? Does lust for power really have to be projected onto a fictive entity? Traditionally, maybe women's lust for power needed excessive camouflage, but was relegation to the Subconscious obligatory? Nowadays, would we consider superheroes to be projections from the comic-book artist's Subconscious? Or would they be commercial products guaranteed to arouse the Subconscious projections of innocent consumers? Or is it a fact that nakedly overt twenty-first century omnipotence fantasies are normal?

"Lizard Near its Snapped-off Tail"

I am now reflecting upon a child who once absorbed the sight of her grandfather, who had returned from WWI with half his face missing. Next she would have spent a few years longing for her father while he was away fighting in WWII. While he was gone, she would have overheard news about the Atomic Bomb and the Holocaust. Eventually, her father returns from a British military hospital where his recovery from shrapnel to the pelvis had taken a very long time. He suffered severe symptoms of "battle fatigue" the rest of his life.

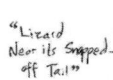

Perhaps this girl had daydreams such as, "If half my face got blasted off, I would just close my good eye and wish wish wish, and my face would grow back like a lizard's tail does." Or perhaps she would dream, "If Hitler came after me I could glare at him so really really hard he'd catapult backwards all the way to the bottom of the Rhine." Or "I wish if an Atom Bomb was dropping on my house, I could just point my finger at it and it would go backwards up into the plane and never blow up." As a grown woman, she probably decided to become a housewife and have 3.2 children, but her cousins Tom, Dick, and Harry might have gone into advertising, public relations, or the audiovisual manufacturing sector.

Witnessing and discovering the same events this little girl did, suppose most North Americans began to feel as vulnerable as a toddler. Suppose apocalypsis induced an unprecedented mass phobia: extreme terror of feeling helpless. Citizens would need heroic denial just to get out of bed every morning, and all the while be desperate for individual power of their own.

The invention of the transistor illustrates the mass effects of the post-apocalyptic omnipotence fantasy. The essential features of this omnipotence fantasy are extremist-grade individualism and mega-sorcerer might. Pure individualism means that trust in communal labour has become as vestigial as the intestinal appendix. Mega-sorcerer might means that a mere wish will make things happen. For so many awestruck victims of apocalypsis, the unexpected result was a sedentary lifestyle.

The transistor emerged from the audio-visual manufacturing sector in the early 1950s. The vision of a transistor began as all technical quests begin: the search for an improvement upon an existing device that is unpredictable, a little messy, too complex, and is large enough to be unwieldy. The invention of a tiny, efficient device that would work more powerfully than the vacuum tube became the centre of ultimate concern for scientists and mass-media industrialists. The transistor would become a brilliant replacement for the vacuum tube, itself a cleverly engineered implement that had made it possible to build radios and eventually televisions ordinary customers could afford. The vacuum tube had amplified and directed a tsunami of electricity so that the great 1946 ENIAC computer could function. The ENIAC had filled a 20 by 40 foot room and used 18,000 vacuum tubes. Realizing what products tinier and tinier transistors could empower, the post-apocalyptic syndrome meshed with, and in a sense defined, twentieth century capitalist dreams. Like the scientists and the industrialists, the consumer was assumed to be someone who was desperate to feel powerful yet too dumbstruck for anything but wishful thinking.

Finally, in 1954 an upgraded transistor enabled the mass-marketed "pocket radio." Compared to the number of vacuum tubes you could fit in your pocket, one, this was a petite radio indeed. This was Year One, Anno Transistorem, first year of the transistor; from then on the sightline for electronics terminated at ultimate power, Egyptian life-force power.

Einstein had never accepted that action at a distance could be real. His word for it was "spooky." Einstein was thinking quantum mechanics, but his adjective invokes the essence of the modern omnipotence fantasy—invisible personal wishes become commands that visible distant objects obey.

For more than half a century now, we can honestly say, "So what?" Since 1960, thanks to transistors, throngs of electrons can readily be policed. The unending rush hour of electrons will obey transistor traffic cops. With electronics, in the New Era of digital technology we get action at a distance galore. A six-week workout with Conor McGregor at MJÖLNIR sports club in Reykjavik isn't necessary if I want the strength to raise and lower a 250-pound garage door five or six times a minute. Muscle has been superseded by remote control electronics. Inside these remote control devices, one or hundreds of teensy-weensy transistors incite whatever superhuman power is needed, such as for satellite navigation of drones, improvised explosive devices, video game consoles, and so forth.

When television channel-changer buttons replaced the television set's channel-change dial, why hadn't people immediately bought a 25-cent length of wood dowelling for pokes at the TV buttons? Instead, we leaned back in our La-Z-Boy, told someone else to change the channel please, and waited for the invention of the TV remote control. With one wee transistor inside it, the TV remote marshals enough juice from a nearby battery to switch on the invisible beam of light that the TV obeys. Everybody scooped up those spooky remotes. A piece of dowelling would have worked faster than standing up and walking over to the TV. Why did that hike seem so painfully slow anyway?

Men have been thrust through space to the moon and back. As many as 128 souls on the Concorde turbojet had been zooming through the atmosphere at speed Mach 2.04. Every time such movements were accomplished the wish to travel as fast as electrons seemed less fanciful. As for drilling down, the Horns Rev wind farm west of Denmark used pile drivers that rammed twenty-five metres deep into the seabed.

Although the twentieth century apocalypses were over, the Collective Subconscious could not eclipse a 1,945-year-old Christian omnipotence fantasy. The power to dig way down and to speed way up were inherent in scripture. "He descended into

Hell; the third day he rose again from the dead." Jesus's tomb was a stairway to Hades; then he flew out of Hades within only three days. Jesus's power and speed survived as an apt paradigm for the twentieth century. For the disciples this would seem an awful lot to occur in only three days. But it's the twenty-first century now. It is taken for granted that airliners departing Helsinki tonight will arrive in Las Vegas within eleven hours.

PHOTOGRAPH TWENTY:
The Grim Reaper

I walked south from the Travelodge to the Eiffel Tower. I would gaze upon it unhurried and with no need to enter Paris Las Vegas, which houses the Tower's two back legs. I had marched up to the Eiffel Tower without the slightest technical knowledge about its construction. My willful ignorance accentuates the Tower's incorrigible material indifference, the fundamental quality of an object-deity. Learning how an object is manufactured might swerve my attention toward human imagination and know-how. The next thing I know I'd be enthralled with engineering details. The next thing I know I'd be admiring the engineers who planned the object. These matters are fascinating and deserve respect. We are given something magnificent to respond to.

According to Niebuhr this encounter is the essence of contemporary polytheism. For him awe is an essential aspect of worship. Niebuhr recognized that great big technologically constructed gods are many and diverse, from the Eiffel Tower in Paris to the Eiffel Tower in Las Vegas. When, according to Niebuhr, we encounter the mysterious sublimity of engineering wonders, this is the last vestige of Christian worship after World War II—unless we pay attention to what the theologians are saying. Niebuhr seems not to have included pure intellectual awe as a symptom of divine presence. Intellectual awe is what we experience all the time in a technological society. Would Niebuhr have counted the Higgs boson particle in his definition of postwar polytheism? The particle is not visually magnificent. Maybe Niebuhr would have OK'd the international space station when it finally landed on a museum in Dubai. Architectural splendors are definitely fascinating but they are not everywhere; they have to be visually massive and elegant to evoke worship; rare indeed on the prairies of Saskatchewan. Mere conceptual mightiness, such as possessed by a nanochip, just does not present a visually glorious span.

If my reading of *Radical Monotheism and Western Culture* hadn't been so lax, maybe I could have deduced Niebuhr's reaction to shopping cart pantheism. Would Niebuhr have realized shopping cart pantheism is truly "new! improved!" over holy monumentality? Or would the onset of shopping cart pantheism be too tacky for words; unlike engineering marvels, shopping cart gods are too accessible to be elite. *Pagan* originally meant "countrified." Shopping cart pantheism is inclusive; urbanites, suburbanites, and rural folk alike couldn't deny the omnipresence of consumer good gods if they tried.

I didn't appreciate the goopy-looking pedestal on which the Tower's two front legs were stabilized. The pedestal looked organic the way pond scum, though glistening with the stillness of green glass, always looks alive. Sludge is not the best foundation for a product deity. The intimation of naturalness, biological viability, or edibility blights any mute otherness that might have been the product's glory. At shoelace level, in contrast, a steel electrical outlet had been jammed into the side of the Tower's pedestal. The predicament of this little god was perversely attractive. It was stuck there, implacable and ugly. And then, there, in the opposite direction were the, oh I don't know, possibly 300,000 faux rivets all along the Tower's legs: they looked like scoops of coconut ice cream. The artificiality was impressive. The artifice was delightful. But these rivets were not convincingly inert. I couldn't trust they were inorganic. Like so many things these days, what if they were another ingenious variant of high-fructose corn syrup?

After watching the electrical outlet not move in its surrounds, my eyes again followed the mock rivets one by one upward. The hot blue sky was the colour of natural gas flame. Up there in the shimmering heat, a chalk-white stone statue on a cornice was leaning across toward the Tower. It was a statue of The Grim Reaper. I tilted my Coolpix toward it for a picture.

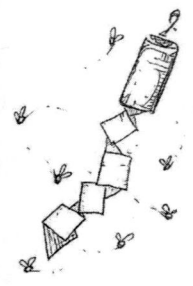

> It is always best
> To look at what lies before our feet,
> For treacherous Time hangs over men
> And twists awry the path of life.[53]

I looked down at the electrical outlet and photographed it too.

"A Bevy oflies Hovering over flypaper"

In *Christianizing the Roman Empire A.D. 100-400*, Ramsay MacMullen noted, "Conversion ... within the non-Christian world did not require doctrine."[54]

I don't consider the imaginings upon which I base shopping cart pantheism to qualify as doctrine. It's way too early for doctrine; it's always way too early for doctrine. For Western tourists Las Vegas is a Mecca of consumable monument moments. At the moment of the economic earthquake of 2008, the tourists were "determined to have a good time. They don't want to hear financial news," and today they do not want doctrine. They have no consciousness of the divine plenitude that swarms around them. Maybe at times something subtly pantheistic will flutter through their nervous system. I am just mentioning that a christianized Subconscious is already laid out like a sheet of flypaper.

Notes

1. Aristotle. *The Poetics*. Section I, Pt. ix.
2. Jaroslav Pelikan. *Christianity and Classical Culture: The Metamorphosis of Natural Theology in the Christian Encounter with Hellenism*. New Haven: Yale UP, 1993. 140.
3. D. W. Winnicott. *Playing and Reality*. London: Penguin, 1986. 15.
4. Winnicott, 91.
5. Paul Tillich. *The Dynamics of Faith*. New York: Harper & Row, 1958. 107.
6. Jean-Paul Sartre. *Existentialism Is a Humanism*. Lecture. 1945.
7. Sigmund Freud. *Civilization and Its Discontents* [*Das Unbehagen in der Kultur*]. Trans. Joan Riviere. London: Hogarth and The Institute of Psycho-Analysis, 1972 [1930]. 6.
8. Firmicus Maternus. *De Errore Profanarum Religionum*. From Harold Mattingly, *Christianity in the Roman Empire*. New York: W. W. Norton, 1967. 92.
9. Ruth Nanda Anshen. "Introduction." World Perspectives Series. Ed. Ruth Nanda Anshen. New York: Harper & Row, 1959.
10. Cindy Crawford. Brainyquote.com/quotes/quotes/c/cindycrawf129532.html#ZU6KHxLvUr3ewvgX.99
11. J. E. Manchip White. *Ancient Egypt: Its Culture and Its History*. New York: Dover, 1970. 34-35.

12. Rudolf Otto. *The Idea of the Holy*. Oxford: Oxford UP, 1958. 205.
13. Rudolf Bultmann. *Existence & Faith*. New York: Meridian, 1960. 203.
14. Bultmann, 181.
15. Tillich, 106.
16. Science.howstuffworks.com/transport/engines-equipment/hydraulic1.htm.
17. Edward Bernays. *Propaganda*. London: Routledge, 1928. 9.
18. Karl Barth. *Dogmatics in Outline*. New York: Philosophical Library, 1949. 7.
19. 1 Samuel 5:6.
20. Pope Benedict XVI. *Introduction to Christianity*. New York: Herder and Herder, 1969.
21. Jean-Paul Sartre. "Bad Faith." *Being and Nothingness*. Trans. Hazel Barnes. New York: Philosophical Library, 1956.
22. Winnicott, 118.
23. Diogenes Laertius. *Lives of the Philosophers*. 7.87.
24. Plotinus. *Enneads*. 6.9.7.
25. Pelikan, 150.
26. Dietrich Bonhoeffer. *Life Together*. New York: Harper & Row, 1954. 96.
27. W. K. C. Guthrie. *The Greeks and Their Gods*. Boston: Beacon, 1955. 240.
28. Guthrie, 240.
29. Matthew 15:10-20.

30. Pindar. *Odes*. Isthmian VIII, Pt. II, lines 14-15. Trans. C. W. Bowra. London: Penguin, 1969. 51.
31. H. Richard Niebuhr, 51.
32. François Genoud, ed. *The Testament of Adolf Hitler: The Hitler-Bormann Documents, February-April 1945.* London: Cassell, 1961.
33. John Kenneth Galbraith. *The Affluent Society*. London: Hamish Hamilton, 1958. 201.
34. Galbraith, 226.
35. Freud, 53.
36. Eands.caltech.edu/articles/LXVI4/brainworms.htm.
37. Robert McAfee Brown. Introduction. *Portrait of Karl Barth*. By Georges Casalis. Garden City: Doubleday, 1963. xv.
38. Martin Buber. *Eclipse of God*. New York: Harper & Row, 1957. 68.
39. Buber, 14.
40. Buber, 72.
41. Buber, 73.
42. Buber, 34.
43. Stanley J. Grenz, David Guretzki, and Cherith Fee Nordling. *Pocket Dictionary of Theological Terms*. Downers Grove: InterVarsity, 1999. 33.
44. Tillich, 21.
45. Pee-wee Herman in *Pee-wee's Big Adventure*, 1985.
46. Tillich, 107.
47. Acts 13:6-12.

48. Tillich, 25.
49. Tillich, 10.
50. Galbraith, 251.
51. James Shiel. *Greek Thought and the Rise of Christianity.* New York: Barnes & Noble, 1968.
52. Pindar. Isthmian V, lines 14-16. 47.
53. Pindar. Isthmian VIII, Pt. II, lines 14-17. 51.
54. Ramsay MacMullen. *Christianizing the Roman Empire A.D. 100-400.* New Haven: Yale UP, 1984. 21.

Acknowledgements

In the spring of 2011, the Writers' Trust of Canada generously provided me with carefree seclusion at the Berton House Writers' Retreat in Dawson City, Yukon. This book fermented in a season of round-the-clock sunshine.

Then Joanne Bristol and Sigrid Dahle read an early splintered version of the book. We made plans to meet at Eva's Gelato to mull over the ideas together. I forgot to go. Nevertheless, Joanne and Sigrid assured me that persisting with the manuscript would not be a waste of brain.

It was a privilege to spend an evening with Aiden Enns. His meticulous considerations of theology, style, and the difference between good and bad jokes made revisions and elaborations an adventure.

I admire and appreciate the sensitivity, smarts, and verve that the ARP Books team brought to this project: John K. Samson's encouragement, Josina Robb's editorial perspicacity and cheer, Bev Phillips's editing prowess. I thank Mike Carroll for the wit and insight of his book design; the cover is the best possible preface.

Jones Miller, thank you for contributing your inimitable and perfectly attuned illustrations.